BUILDING AN ENDOWMENT RIGHT FROM THE START

By Lynda S. Moerschbaecher

with contributing authors
Barbara G. Hammerman and James C. Soft

Precept Press

05   04   03   02   01   5   4   3   2   1

Library of Congress Cataloging-in-Publication Data

Moerschbaechaer, Lynda S.
    Building an endowment : right from the start / by Lynda S.
Moerschbaecher ; with contributing authors Barbara G. Hammerman and
James Soft.
        p.   cm.
    ISBN 0-944496-68-7
    1. Endowments—Planning.   I. Hammerman, Barbara G.   II. Soft, James.
III. Title.
    HV16 .M52 2001
    658.15'224—dc21   2001001929

Precept Press
Division of Bonus Books, Inc.
160 East Illinois Street
Chicago, Illinois 60611

Printed in the United States of America

Table of Contents

Acknowledgments

Many thanks to Barbara Hammerman and Jim Soft for helping make this work come to fruition. It would not have happened without them.

I also thank Evelyn Brody for her outstanding research in the field of endowment, and especially for giving me the motivation and inspiration to turn my seminar materials into this handbook.

Introduction: Legacy Created

"What are you going to get when your lease expires? I can't imagine you in anything but your Mustang convertible."

"What I would really like is an El Camino," I said, leaning my arm into Clarke's space at the bar. Duartes Tavern was really packed that night, a hundred years old and full of the same locals, or so it seemed. Maybe some tourists, too. Halfway between Santa Cruz and San Francisco is a certain spot on Earth that attracts both.

So I confessed my long-held desire to have an El Camino, but they stopped making them in 1987 and I hadn't really made an effort to get a used one. I kept saying, "Someday."

Clarke had been around the locale for about as long as the bar was there. He looked up and down the length of it and said in his quiet, grizzled manner, looking back at the whiskey in front of him, "Joe's got an El Camino."

Being relatively new to town, I asked, "Who's Joe?"

Clarke cocked his head and sidled a glance at me that said, "Whaddya mean, who's Joe?"

"He's right down there at the end of the bar." I leaned past Clarke to see if I could pick him out. There was a group engaged in convivial conversation, no doubt about the artichoke crop or the recent flooding.

Joe Gianinni stopped his conversation when Clarke leaned his head in the way of my view and shouted over the din, "Hey, Joe, you still got that El Camino?"

Joe's a retired farmer and local icon who doesn't give anything up he doesn't have to. He dipped his head in a deep nod over his nightly Tuaca Italian Coffee — two to be exact, never one or three — and responded slowly and with great certainty in a mellifluous Italian-tinged voice, "Yes, I have The Camino."

Clarke turned excitedly to me and repeated what I already heard. "Joe has The Camino, so what year are you looking for?"

"Of course, the 1986. The year before they quit making it was the best, a really good runner."

Clarke swung his head to the left in full action now, sailing his words down to the end of the bar, "Hey Joe. What year's that Camino?"

"It's an '86, but I want to sell it." The words hung in the air over me. Clarke leaned forward again blocking my view of Joe. "Well, imagine that. This lady to my right wants to buy one."

That set the stage for the most curious and enjoyable transaction that I can ever remember. Outside Duartes the rain had been falling for days, but now decided to be a veritable deluge. Inside, the warmth of the place and the friendliness seemed to render the rain harmless, even though we all knew the Pescadero and San Gregorio Creeks were about to pit resident against nature and make feuding and loving townsfolk caretakers of one another. That's just how it is in small agricultural towns.

Clarke slipped off his stool and I hastened to follow. He introduced me to Joe. Joe stared at me for a moment, reading what he saw and pulled the car key out of his pocket. He slipped it to me and said, "Take 'er for a spin and see what you think."

I hadn't known Joe for 50 seconds and he gave me the keys to The Camino. Clarke and I went out in the downpour to see her, but I declined a ride. A test drive when you can't see the street is not wise. But even through the rain, I couldn't help noticing the glorious 1986, two-tone gold and brown El Conquista in pristine condition. Clarke said Joe rarely left the area any more except to visit his son up the road, his grandson in Half Moon Bay or to go down to Castroville to his artichoke farm.

I did a full tour around the car and knew this thing was going to be part of my life. I did not know what part of the community it already was. We went back into the tavern and I handed Joe the keys. I asked if I could come by the next day to drive it. His response was to tell me the price. Fair, reasonable, in fact, I had the feeling that I wouldn't dream of dickering with him because it was my privilege to pay him money for this opportunity. What was coming over me? The involuntary "feel good" response was overtaking me.

Joe told me he had had the car since it was brand new and that he always loved her. But his grandson wanted to buy him a new truck. I felt his remorse in parting with her, but I could sense it was also important to accept something his grandson wanted to do for him. He invited me to his house the next day to drive El Conquista.

The next day at 10 a.m., as planned, I made my way over to North Street, the downtown residential section of Pescadero. As I pulled up to his one-story stucco home with pebble lawn and statuary, Joe greeted me warmly and introduced me to his wife, Mary. After the requisite pleasantries, Joe let me take The Camino for a drive. What a dream, big seats, pristine, cared for, quality.

I took her out the back roads, onto the highway and I began to wonder about Joe and Mary. The car seemed full of good feelings. I got back to Joe's and parked in front of the house and notice the glassine cover on the visor holding the registration. P.O. Box 1, Pescadero, California. This is a town that has been around since the 1870s. They've been here a long, long time.

Pleasantries exchanged, I stated my intent to buy the vehicle. I was ready to pull out my checkbook. But Joe asked me to come back the next day to have coffee with him and Mary and he would have the paperwork ready. I thought, okay, I am not in a hurry. I still had my Mustang convertible and I would enjoy seeing Joe and Mary again.

The next morning as I entered the house, Mary greeted me at the door as if I were there every day at this time for coffee. We went to a sitting room table off the kitchen. Joe and Mary and I sat cozily near a window and I admired Mary's garden. I accepted the coffee.

"Would you like a little Amaretto in your coffee?" Joe asked invitingly.

At 10:30 a.m. I had not yet developed a taste for libation of that sort and politely declined. Joe looked disappointed. We chatted a little more and I expected the paperwork to be forthcoming at any moment. Instead, Joe reached around behind him and pulled out some photos, a beautiful photo of him and Mary when she was barely past mid-teens and he was a strapping 21-year-old fresh from Italy. The spark in their eyes then was mirrored in their eyes as I looked at them. Joe spoke of their courtship and poured me more coffee. He renewed his invitation to have a little Amaretto in my coffee. Again I declined.

Again I detected disappointment, so I said, "Oh, why not, sure, I'd love some." I was rewarded with a huge grin and Joe pulled out his car folder. He placed the papers on the table in front of us and proclaimed, "Ah, NOW we talk about The Camino."

I unwittingly participated in a test that I almost failed, but after a couple of wrong answers, I finally got it. Joe fingered the papers as if they were birth certificates of his children. We filled them out and he passed the file folder over to me.

As we walked toward the front door, his pace slowed and I could feel his reluctance to part with his Camino El Conquista. I offered that if he did not want to give it up and had second thoughts, I would understand. He clasped his hands to his chest and exclaimed, "Oh, no. Mary and I want you to have The Camino." His smiling eyes said yes, it was indeed so.

We posed next to the car for some photos. Mary lingered at the door and waved at me, on and on, as I drove up the street in Joe's car. I paused at the stop sign before turning right on North Street and the neighbors at the corner offered a familiar wave in my direction until they noticed that Joe was not at the wheel. Their heads did a full rotation looking to see who was driving Joe's car.

In another half mile, I stopped to turn right onto Pescadero Road. Someone turning from Pescadero onto North lifted his hand from the wheel in the time-honored acknowledgment of neighbors greeting neighbors in a small town. It's a good thing no one was behind me that he could hit, because he swerved viciously when he realized someone else was driving Joe's car.

Two other "who-the-heck-was-that" looks hit me before I got safely to my driveway. But by the time I got there I felt I had made several new friends. That was just the beginning.

That night at Duarte's, Joe came up to me and said, "Hey, Miss Barbara, I got another key here."

Bill rushed up to me, "So you're the one that got Joe's car? I've been trying to buy that for years." Joe smiled slyly and said in his velvet Italian voice, "She's prettier than you, Bill."

The next day at the gas station (I mean The gas station in town), a tall gentleman came up and said, "That Joe's car?" I replied bravely, "No, it's mine, well, it was Joe's."

He scrutinized me getting ready to pump gas, looked down upon me and said, "Use THIS gas in Joe's car, that's what he uses." "Thank you, of course."

The next day in the window seat of Regie's diner, I was admiring my Camino. Someone burst in to the diner and said, "Where's Joe?" looking around in a puzzled manner.

Regie said, "Oh, Joe's not here, that's Barbara's car now," pointing to me.

The man looked at me tentatively and said, "I hope you don't mind me asking, but where you gonna get the car serviced?" I knew I had only the wrong answer, I could tell right away. Having it serviced in Half Moon Bay where I got the Mustang serviced was not going to work.

He furrowed his brow, reached up and absent-mindedly rubbed the back of his neck as I took altogether too long to answer. So he answered for me, "Well, Joe always takes it to Sarabia. Sarabia knows the car, knows what to do, ya know?" I got the distinct idea that this was not idle conversation; this was a mandate.

"Thank you, of course." This refrain had become my mantra of late.

Joe has now taken to introducing me around the community. It's not just Barbara, but Barbara-who-has-The-Camino-now. Sort of like, Barbara-to-whom-we-have-just-given-our-first-born, and with a tinge of longing, but quiet calm and pleasure, "Mary and I are happy she has The Camino."

Over a year later, Joe still asks, "You still have the Camino, don't you?" I always assure him yes. He always invites me over to see him and Mary.

At the gas station, I say, "Joe's car needs a fill-up."

At Sarabia, I say, "Can you put a new battery in Joe's car today?"

At the car wash, I say I'm going to get Joe's car cleaned up. The lady in the market told me which car wash to go to.

As I dropped off the trash at our local transfer station, the boy said, "Cool car. Is it yours?"

I paused for a second, but not too long and said, "Kinda. It's mine and Joe's." The feeling of community is embodied in the statement and the realization that it takes a village to love a car. It's the investment in the community and the community's investment in it. It is shared common values and ideals, a knowing that people care, and they care very, very much about Joe, Mary, the car, the community. Just like helping each other in the flood, but every day in their own way, whether or not the artichoke fields, farms and houses are drenched in water.

* * * * * * *

How this legacy was created and perpetuated made the authors realize a lot about their chosen professions. What people give to their community is much like Joe's car. It builds and builds. And they choose very carefully to whom they will give it away. Like giving the "records of the births of their children" when Joe and Mary gave the title to their car, they give deeds to homes and stock in their long-held companies or long-favored investments. But they never give it away. You know they don't. It is part of them and they are part of it forever. They share. What is ownership anyway? Nothing but stewardship.

Stewardship, as in old England, where the sty warden (the origin of the word), one who guards the pig sty on behalf of someone else, was a valuable, honorable position. And that's what we do when we hold endowment funds. Our organizations hold *their* property, kinda. It's "Joe's and mine." We hold it and they accept our holding of it, as long as we do right by it and them.

What more important could we possibly say about the creation of a legacy through the holding of an endowment? It is a sacred fiduciary duty to the community, whatever that community is: local, regional, national, international, geographic or nongeographic. All the principles in Joe's story hold true for us in endowment fundraising. Right down to accepting the Amaretto in the coffee to make the deal happen. What is important to them should be of utmost importance to us. To create this legacy, we must respect their thoughts and beliefs of what is right and work to preserve them the best we can, especially in light of changing circumstances.

This whole handbook is based on this premise. How to build it *right*, from the very start. And keep it that way.

1

Endowment Perspectives

In the 25 years the authors have been in the business of nonprofit fundraising, more times than not we have found that simply because an organization's Board of Directors is enthusiastic about a new fundraising strategy, it does not mean the board members will be open to the process that comes with it. Because boards tend toward immediacy once a course of action is determined, lessons about the keys to fundraising success are learned the hard way.

This scenario often begins with an approach that says, "We need an endowment. Go do it." You know, of course, board members do not necessarily want to help you do it once you've been given your marching orders. They may not even want to fund the project. They don't want to send you to class, and they don't want to hear about a lengthy time frame. But they do *really* want that endowment. And they want to know how much you are going to raise, and when.

So you begin this monumental task with few resources, little support and even less time. In the pages ahead you will discover how to overcome these pressures and learn the process of setting up and securing an endowment fund. We will examine where

1

money comes from, where it goes and how it grows. We will set forth rules and guidelines for its management. We will unlock and outline the ways in which an endowment can become a most effective fundraising investment.

Endowment is an easy word, but you cannot imagine how much punch is packed into it. Before starting this book, we called several endowment consultants to see what should be covered in a day-long seminar or a book. One commented, "How can you talk about endowment for a day? I can tell you everything I know in just a few minutes." But as we talked, he realized that what he knew about endowment he learned over many years and it simply had gotten assimilated into his knowledge: policies, investments, legal, management, board, etc. Those who know a lot about endowments forget that there is much more to it than "hold the principal, spend the income."

What about those others who are trying to get their endowments established? How do they learn? Well, some learn the hard way. About five years ago a client called one of the authors in panic. "I really need to talk to you," he said, "because a donor is insisting that I give his money back." Before being asked, the client insisted he didn't do anything wrong. He explained that a donor gave him $5,000 and later claimed he wasn't using the money properly and asked that the money be returned. Certainly one could sympathize with the client, but it is likely that there was some misunderstanding.

The client said he requested a major gift and received $5,000. He also claimed he never specified how the money would be used. According to the client, however, the donor insisted the organization should only be using the income from his $5,000 gift. The client said the gift came in response to a special brochure appeal for what his organization called, "Our Endowment Campaign." On being asked if he knew what endowment is, it became immediately clear that he had confused two very distinct concepts — major gifts and endowment. A major gift *may* be one that can be spent immediately while an endowment is held in perpetuity.

This client's confusion did not come as a great surprise. Shortly after completing law school, one of the authors went to work for an organization with the third highest ranked endowment in the country. Being fairly young and still unclear about a few concepts, she thought walking around the large development office asking people about endowment was probably the best way to learn about the subject. She never really got a very succinct definition or explanation of how it works, and soon discovered there were many people in fundraising who shared this lack of understanding.

Since then, this has become a mission of understanding and articulating the concept of endowment, all the authors having led nationally-recognized seminars on this topic for more than 15 years. This book is an outgrowth of the demand for these seminars and features the essential aspects — from law application to accounting rules — associated with understanding and executing this procedure properly and effectively. After reading this book, you will not only have a solid grasp of what endowment is and how it works, you will be ready to *build an endowment right from the start*.

Historical Perspectives

Endowments are anything but new. They have existed since at least the eleventh and twelfth centuries. In her wonderful article in the *Arizona Law Review* (39 Ariz. L. Rev. 873, 1997), Evelyn Brody, Assistant Professor of Law, Chicago-Kent School of Law, states:

> Over the centuries, the secularization and democratization of support for charity enlarged the conception of who qualifies to manage a charity, as well as who qualifies as a beneficiary. In medieval England, making a gift to the poor was part of practicing religion, and the bishops and priests administered charity. The twelfth and thirteenth centuries brought a host of hospital foundations by private benefactors: "Kings, bishops, feudal lords, wealthy merchants, guilds, and municipalities all endowed houses of charity." Medieval "hospitals" included general almshouses for "indoor" (resident) and "outdoor" (doles and pensions) poor relief, homes for the old and invalid, orphanages, lying-in hospitals, and leper colonies. More than 600 such institutions existed in England by the middle of

the fourteenth century. A papal decree on hospital law, issued in 1311, provided an explicit statement on the inviolability of the charity's resources. The decretal established a procedure for bishops merely to audit hospital administration, and explicitly determined that the wardenship of a hospital did not constitute an ecclesiastical benefice.

However, society in any given time did not always agree as to the benefit or need for endowments. Nor did they agree as to how to save or spend the money. These debates continue to this date and probably will not cease any time soon.

In 1536 in English law, The Statute of Uses gave in to a common use not condoned by the government, regarding an arrangement we now know as trusts. What had developed was a practice whereby one who desired to transfer of land to someone other than the oldest son created an arrangement giving title to another (third) person for the benefit of those who could not hold legal title. This "user" of property was often incapable of holding title to property due to various incapacities in the law, such as being a woman or a criminal. Thus, the transferor had to "trust" the title holder, becoming the "trustor" and gave the property to the third party, the "trustee" or trusted one, "for the benefit of" the nontitleholders. These latter parties became the "beneficiaries."

In 1601, English law also enacted the Elizabethan Statute of Charitable Uses, only to be followed by disputes over who got what funds, such as increases in rents and access to principal, or whether heirs had any right to claim against surpluses. Charity was generally given the right to such increases in value.

Ms. Brody cites the following case on endowments as a result of this law:

> The School of Thetford's Case upon a Bill exhibited in Parliament, 8 Jac. 8 Coke fol. 130. Land of the value of 35 l. by the year, was, by Sir Thomas Fulmerston 9 Eliz. Devised to certin persons in Trust, and their heirs, for maintenance of a Preacher, Schoolmaster, and poor People, in Thetford, and by the Will, a special distribution was made, how much the Preacher, Schoolmaster, and Poor should have, amounting in the whole unto 35 l. by the year, which was the value of the Land at the time of the Devise, and afterwards the Land in-

creaseth to be by the value of 100 l. by the year, and upon a Reference to the Chief Justices, and Judge Walmsley, they certified their opinions, that the Revenue of the Lands shall be imployed to increase the several stipends of the persons appointed to be maintained by the Devise, and if any surplusage do remain, it shall be imployed for the maintainance of a great number of people, and nothing shall be converted by the Devisees, to their own use, for that it appeareth by the distribution of the Devisor, that he intended that all the Profits of his Lands, shall be imployed in the Charitable Works by him funded, and left nothing to his Heirs or Executors, of the Profits of his Lands, as they were in value at his death, and as if the value of the Land had decreased, the Poor should have lost in their stipends, so when the Revenue of the Lands increase, they shall gain; and the Lord Coke said, That this Resolution did concern all the Colledges in the Universities, and elsewhere; for when the Lands were first given for their maintainance, and that every Scholar should have a Pennyhalfepenny a day, this was then a competent allowance for a Scholar, in respect of the price of Victuals then, and yearly value of the Land, and now the price of Victuals being increased, the first maintainance for Scholars, is not competent for them; and as the value of the Lands increase, so ought the Allowance for the Scholars to increase; for the Colledges seized in Jure Collegii, to the intent, that the Members of the Colledge shall be maintained, according to the intent of the Founder, which is, that all the Revenue and Increase of the Profits of their Lands, shall be bestowed in the Works of Charity, which the Founder hath expressed, and that nothing should be committed to any other private uses, for panis egentum est vita pauperum, & qui defraudat eos homo sanguinis est, and upon conference with all the Judges of England, they agreed to the Opinion of both the aforesaid Judges, and both Houses of Parliament passed the Bill accordingly, and the King assented to the Bill.

In 1736, England passed a law called the Modern Law of Mortmain, the preamble to which perhaps addresses societal concerns at the time:

Whereas gifts or alienations of lands, tenements, or hereditaments in Mortmain, are prohibited or restrained by Magna

Charta and divers other wholsome laws, as prejudicial to and against the common utility; nevertheless this publick mischief has of late greatly increased by many large and improvident alienations or dispositions made by languishing or dying persons, or by other persons, to uses called Charitable uses, to take place after their death, to the disherison of their lawful heirs.

The law of 1736 did not permit any transfers of land at death for any charitable purpose. In addition, a lifetime gift to charity had to be made outright and absolutely, at least twelve months before the donor's death, and enrolled in the chancery court within six months of execution (similar to admitting it to Probate court). The basic Mortmain statutes were not repealed until 1960. It should be no surprise then that England does not enjoy the same planned and endowment giving the charities do in the United States. One of the authors visited with a charitable bequest firm in England in 1997 to discuss the state of charitable giving through trusts, since the current American version of trusts began with the Statute of Uses in England in the sixteenth century. Apparently, little or no such giving is being promoted, but the firm expressed much interest in learning how to go about setting up such trusts. Unfortunately, the tax laws give no incentives as the U.S. laws do for such trusts. Bequests are therefore far more popular, according to the firm.

The English laws of Mortmain did not apply to the American colonies and thus the American concept of charitable endowments and foundations developed along their own lines, not without controversy, however. In the nineteenth century, The Supreme Court urged states to adopt statutes similar to the English law "to prevent undue influence and imposition upon pious and feeble minds in their last moments, and to check that unhappy propensity which sometimes is found to exist under a bigoted enthusiasm, and the desire to gain fame as a religious devotee and benefactor, at the expense of all the natural claims of blood and parental duty to children."

Others strongly urged laws to limit the life of charitable trusts and foundations for a period of years, such as 25 or 40, or at least to have a period of inviolability when the mandate of the founder would be followed. After that, the foundation or trust would be administered in accordance with the then current needs.

The debate continued for years, into the twentieth century. Sears founder Julius Rosenwald published an essay in *Atlantic Monthly* creating a sensation in 1929.

> There are few colleges in the land today which are not striving for "adequate endowment." Museums, orchestras, operas, homes for the aged, hospitals, orphanages, and countless other charitable and remedial organizations, are aiming at the same goal. It was recently estimated that more than two and a half billion dollars were given to various endowments in this country in the last fifteen years. The sum is vast, equal to the total national wealth a hundred years ago, but institutions continue to solicit more and greater endowments, and men of wealth are encouraging them with ever-increasing gifts.

> "All of this giving and receiving," Rosenwald lamented, "is proceeding without much, if any, attention to the underlying question whether perpetual endowments are desirable."

Rosenwald did not believe in perpetual endowments and limited his foundation to a term of years. Brody cites another similar view of that time period:

> A few shared Rosenwald's principles. Baron de Hirsch's will preferred preserving capital, but permitted the trustees, by written two-thirds agreement, to spend from capital if necessary to "adequately" carry out the trust's purposes, but not for the first ten years, "and in such cases only for the purpose of the purchase of land and the erection of buildings for schools..., and not more than ten per cent of the capital shall be expended in any year." Deed of Trust of the Baron de Hirsch Fund, Jan. 22, 1891, arts. 8 & 9, in Legal Instruments of Foundations, supra note 18, at 85, 89. The 1945 will of Emil Schwarzhaupt imposed a 25-year life on his foundation, and forbid paying Foundation funds into any endowment. Last Will and Testament of Emil Schwarzhaupt, signed Dec. 19, 1945, art. 11, in Legal Instruments of Foundations, supra note 18, at 73, 77 ("in the long run society is benefitted by having

each generation solve its own problems and provide the necessary funds for so doing, and...endowments, in order to be responsive to the ideals, wishes and needs of each respective generation, should be created by such generation").

Two general types of donor restrictions concerned Julius Rosenwald. The first were those given for a narrow purpose, which, inevitably, outlive the exigencies of their era. Second, Rosenwald wrote of the "endowment poor" institutions, and the resulting harm to society: "Research suffers; museums are unable to purchase objects that never again will be available; experiments of all sorts are frowned upon, not because they do not promise well, but because money to undertake anything out of the ordinary cannot be found, while huge sums are regularly budgeted to carry on traditional and routine activities." Against the argument that endowments tide organizations over hard times, he asserted that those "are precisely the times when it is most important to have unrestricted funds which will permit our institutions to continue their work until conditions improve, as they always do."

Rosenwald blamed the timidity of the trustees themselves for their inability to spend principal. "Donors would in many cases be willing to give greater discretion to trustees in such matters if they were asked to do so." Indeed, in the course of working with charities, Rosenwald observed how "funds given with no strings attached have been added to the perpetual endowment as a matter of course." Rosenwald saves some of the blame for knee-jerk drafting by lawyers, who "have not learned that money can be given in any other way." Rosenwald acknowledged the donor's desire for a lasting memorial — "an end which becomes increasingly attractive to many men with advancing years" — but reminds us that nothing endures. Indeed, perpetuities express a lack of confidence in trustees, who "are told that they are wise enough and honest enough to invest the money and spend the income amounting to 4 to 5 percent each year; but they are told in the same breath that they are not capable of spending 6 to 10 or 15 percent wisely." Perhaps worse, perpetuities encourage the build-up of bureaucracies — of course, this sinecure might explain why trustees put up with the insult of limited confidence....

All of this giving and receiving, Rosenwald lamented, is proceeding without much, if any, attention to the underlying question whether perpetual endowments are desirable.

In the early 1900s, Congress' Commission on Industrial Relations believed that the concentration of wealth in the large foundations, such as Carnegie and Rockefeller, was being used by industrial magnates to gain control of the universities and, thereby, the social and educational side of American life. If only they had seen what resurgence there has been in the creation of foundations, some very large, as a result of the technology sector wealth of the last few years. Except this time it is not only concentrated in a few large foundations; it is widespread in multimillion to multibillion dollar foundations that are springing up all over the nation from sudden high-tech wealth that are reshaping the educational and cultural landscape of today and tomorrow.

For the serious student of endowments and endowment history, the Evelyn Brody article in the *Arizona Law Review* is a must. It is over 90 pages long and traces much of the history, legislation, practice and policy disputes over endowments. This and other of her writings are highly recommended and enjoyable reading.

Current Perspectives

Who has endowments and what are they worth? And perhaps more importantly, how do you find such information? There are few public sources available to learn and compare which organizations have endowments and how developed those endowments are. Many organizations now have websites where they post their own endowment figures, but as of this writing there seem to be no centralized sources for comparison of many of them. NACUBO (National Association of College and University Business Officers), located in Washington, D.C. conducts a survey of voluntarily participating colleges and universities, with the assistance of Cambridge Associates, an endowment consulting company. The results are reported each year and may be obtained through the website, *www.nacubo.org*. Results reported in the 1999 NACUBO Study are summarized as follows:

Of the 509 institutions that participated in the survey for the 1999 report, endowment was reported at $195 billion, up from $150.2 billion reported by 461 institutions in 1997. This is just a number of colleges, universities and schools — it does not include all other types of institutions!

Of that number, 129 (26% of reporting institutions) have endowments of $300 million or more and control 80+% of the endowment money. Of those, *a mere 34 institutions*, 7% of them, have assets in excess of $1 billion and represent over half of the total endowments.

In 1997, 79 institutions controlled 71% of that dollar amount, or $106.5 billion, leaving $44.7 billion in the hands of the rest of the reporting institutions. Currently, Harvard has the highest endowment for private institutions, at $14.26 billion (up from $10.9 billion in 1997) and the University of Texas has the highest for a public institution, at $8 billion (up from $6.7 billion in 1997). Harvard also had $732 million in life income gifts and UT had $23 million. The lowest level organization in the list reported approximately $5.8 million in 1999 while in 1997, the lowest reported $3 million in endowments.

In 1996, Philanthropic Research Institute, an organization that is hard to locate now (possibly a part of *Guidestar.com*), surveyed 42,000 organizations, of which 6,000 had endowments. A sample of 820 of these done by Evelyn Brody, author of "Charitable Endowments and the Democratization of Dynasty" (39 Ariz. Law Review), discovered that the endowments ran from minuscule to those capable of supporting the organization for up to 50 years without additional income.

Of those capable of support for two years or more without additional income, approximately 26% were museums, libraries, zoos, gardens, symphonies and other cultural institutions, 20% were community foundations, 23% were hospitals, medical research and children's or adult homes, 7% were Boy Scouts, YMCA, 4-H or fraternal charities, 7% academic research or schools, 13% were humane societies, a handful were retirement homes for various congregations or Jewish charities and others were unclassifiable on the basis of their name.

Additional information can be gleaned from IRS data in the Statistics of Income reports that are issued periodically by the IRS, called the SOI Bulletin. This may be found at their website, *www.irs.gov*. Tax information gathered from returns is analyzed and reported, along with some very interesting studies, several of nonprofits in recent years. The most current analyses, however, are pulled from tax returns of several years ago. Current reports for the year 2000 are based on returns that range from about 1995 to 1998.

Tax data from 1993 (latest information available on this point from the SOI) show that public charities held $421.5 billion in investments (not necessarily endowment, but non-operating assets). This was comprised of $320.7 billion in securities, $18.3 billion in investment real estate and $82.5 billion in other passive investments. Small charities filing the 990-EZ Form reported $1 billion additional in cash, savings and investments. TIAA-CREF was still exempt at that time and held about $126.5 billion, leaving about $296 billion in the hands of charities.

In addition, private foundations held $195 billion in 1993. Current reports show the 2% tax on investment income to be $500,000. This would likely translate into $250,000,000 of investment income. This would further translate into an amount approaching $300–400 billion in assets. Churches are not required to file with the IRS, so no information is available on them. Consider the extent of assets held by them added to the available numbers.

IRS figures from 1975 to 1995 data also show that revenue and assets of nonprofits tripled from $0.9 trillion to $1.9 trillion (adjusted for inflation and therefore a real increase) during that 20-year period.

2

Operational Aspects

To many people, the concept of endowment means a source of funds for the operation of a charitable entity. Endowment, however, is a restriction on the *use* of funds and has nothing to do with the generation of those funds. Every nonprofit has certain ways to generate revenue and certain ways in which it can use that revenue. Let's look at those ways from the perspective of sources and uses of nonprofit funds.

Sources of Revenue

Every nonprofit has five potential legally available sources of revenue and no more (as illustrated in the chart below). Some nonprofits utilize all of these sources, others only some. Actual revenue production programs may be broken into different classifications than listed here or be named differently than here, but these are the basic ways an organization can generate revenue for its existence. The revenue production area called fundrais-

NONPROFIT REVENUE — ALL SOURCES

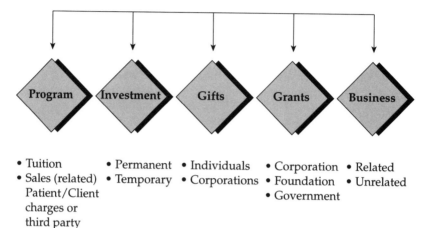

Program	Investment	Gifts	Grants	Business
• Tuition	• Permanent	• Individuals	• Corporation	• Related
• Sales (related) Patient/Client charges or third party reimbursements	• Temporary	• Corporations	• Foundation • Government	• Unrelated
• Admissions				

ing comprises two parts of the five possible revenue production areas.

At the far left side of the chart, you will note that one of these sources is program fees. What does the charter of the organization permit or perhaps mandate as its charitable activities? If those exempt-function activities generate revenue, that is program revenue. For example, a school charges tuition, a hospital charges patient fees or receives third party reimbursements, a museum may charge admissions, a nonprofit thrift store may have sales of merchandise related to its exempt purpose. All of those are revenues derived from the conduct of a program or programs, the purpose for which the organization exists.

If you look at the opposite side of the chart, you will see another possible source of revenue, in the nature of a trade or business. Not every organization engages in this type of activity. If the organization engages in a trade or business, and if the trade or business is related, the income derived from it will not be taxable. If it engages in a trade or business unrelated to the purpose for which the charity exists and does so on a regular basis, that is taxable as unrelated business income. If such is the case, then the organization is competing in the marketplace with other businesses offering the same goods or services that are taxed on their revenues. Unfair competition by nonprofits gave rise to the creation and imposition of the unrelated business income tax in the 1950s.

The classic example of this is the 1950s case of the Mueller Macaroni Company, which was owned by New York University. The company's ownership was obviously the root of the problem, and it was from this case that the unrelated business income rules emerged. Many companies, including Mueller's competitors in the macaroni industry, complained that NYU was noodling (pun intended) them out of business. Their concern was that NYU was taking unfair advantage of its tax-exempt status by competing in the marketplace, in a business unrelated to its function, without having to pay taxes on its profits. That is fundamentally the opposite of educating students and charging them tuition (program revenue).

Between these two extremes on the above chart are, for the most part, activities, or the result of the activities, of the fundraising office. You may wish to go further in analyzing the five sources of nonprofit revenue than just understanding conceptually that they exist. In fact, you may be in for some interesting surprises if you use this chart to analyze your own organization's actual dollar allocation both for revenue received and expenses allocated among these five revenue sources for the last three to five years. You may even begin to note some important trends and shifts from year to year.

Generally, financial records are not kept on this basis, so a little work needs to be done to categorize the revenues in this manner. The result, however, is likely to be a better understanding of your starting point for any new program in any one of these five categories. Be sure you either use gross amount, before expenses for all categories, or net amounts for all categories, so that you are comparing apples with apples. Using the net amounts is preferable because you will readily see what the effort is really worth in each category to the nonprofit.

Occasionally consultants joke to Boards of Directors that the fundraising effort pays such a high net on the gross revenue received in the two applicable categories (grants and gifts), that they should consider abandoning the carrying out of the nonprofit program and just undertake fundraising.

FIVE REVENUE SOURCES OF
THE DEVELOPMENT OFFICE

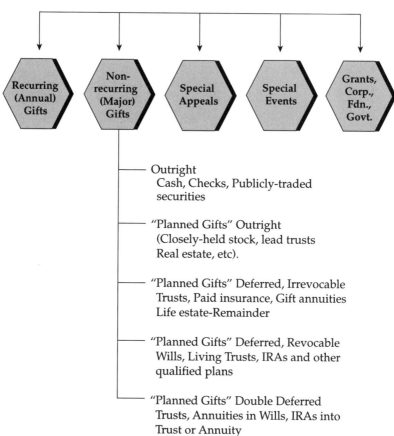

Recurring (Annual) Gifts

Non-recurring (Major) Gifts

Special Appeals

Special Events

Grants, Corp., Fdn., Govt.

— Outright
Cash, Checks, Publicly-traded
securities

— "Planned Gifts" Outright
(Closely-held stock, lead trusts
Real estate, etc).

— "Planned Gifts" Deferred, Irrevocable
Trusts, Paid insurance, Gift annuities
Life estate-Remainder

— "Planned Gifts" Deferred, Revocable
Wills, Living Trusts, IRAs and other
qualified plans

— "Planned Gifts" Double Deferred
Trusts, Annuities in Wills, IRAs into
Trust or Annuity

Revenue from *gifts* derives from programs within the development office designed to acquire revenue from existing or newly acquired donors. Revenue from gifts and grants can be broken into five further subsets; revenue specifically from the development office is shown on the chart just above as a breakout below the five sources of nonprofit revenue. Development programs are efforts directed in different manners to achieve the same goal: obtaining gratuitous funding, without offering anything in return, to assist in keeping the organization operational. It is important to keep in mind that each of the various types of revenue production programs has a common goal. Lack of understanding of this common goal is the source of many woes in the development office. Every well-rounded development office has established programs in these five areas, even though all of them may be staffed by only one or two people.

Looking closer at revenue from the breakout of gifts and grants on the development office chart just above, what is the difference between a gift and a grant as a source of development revenue (looking only where the money comes from). When a donor makes a gift, he or she gives up control. The tax law calls it "detached and disinterested generosity." In other words, the donor does not retain a financial interest, it is voluntary or gratuitous (even though perhaps earmarked for a special use), whereas grants from a foundation, corporation or government agency often come with spending stipulations or parameters more like a contract. A certain quid pro quo expectation often arises in regard to how the grant funds are to be spent.

Think for a moment about the donor in the circumstance of a grant and a gift. Who is the donor of this grant? He or she is in fact a sophisticated buyer in the donee marketplace. He or she is a sophisticated purchaser of nonprofit goods or services. The granting organization is giving money in exchange for the nonprofit performing a particular function. As purchasers of the services, they know exactly what they are doing.

How sophisticated is that individual gift market? Who is the donor? While the donor may know a little bit about a major gift or may have learned a bit about a life income gift, he or she is, for the most part, not in the business of giving money away. The frequency with which the individual donor gives money or property away pales in comparison to the grant-making foundation or corporate philanthropic office. If the individual donors are amateurs — or, unsophisticated buyers of your services — they are usually giving a pure gift of "detached and disinterested generosity."

So, when you're thinking about sources of revenue and where they come from in the fundraising effort, this may be a good way to distinguish between gifts and grants. Generally, grants are not made for endowment. The sophisticated "purchasers" in the donee market expect the funds to be used currently to accomplish the charitable purpose in question. Individuals are more likely to give to endowment and consider the future.

In the last of the five sources of revenue of a nonprofit (the chart above), the investment area is money either temporarily parked from surplus of any of these five revenue sources, or money permanently invested as a result of gifts where the principal is not expended, only income or some form of it. This is called endowment.

End Use of Revenue Received

As we turn to the end uses of nonprofit revenue, remember that nonprofits often use names for revenue programs that in fact indicate the end use of funds once obtained, for example, capital campaign or endowment campaign. There is nothing inherently wrong with doing this, as long as the development professional understands the clear definitions of these terms. Too often, new development staff is not educated as to what is revenue versus what is use of gifted funds. A brief nonprofit accounting course for those at the outset of employment as a development officer, management or board member would serve the organization well.

In order to understand the difference between revenue generation and revenue uses, let us look at the three ways of spending gifted funds and see how the five sources of nonprofit revenue feed into these three uses of funds.

Three End Uses of Funds

There are only three ways to spend nonprofit revenue: 1) operationally in the carrying out of the organization's program, 2) on capital projects (land, buildings, improvements and equipment) or 3) by restricting it to endowment.

Operational expenditures hardly need a discussion here. Nor do capital spending projects, which account for bricks and mortar projects like land, improvements and buildings. However, endowment is often poorly understood, even among fundraisers. We need to examine endowment as an end use of funds and how it relates to gift revenue source.

When an organization prepares to have a capital campaign, capital refers to the end use of funds, and campaign to the fundraising effort. The same is true for an endowment campaign. There is one exception — there is an actual definition of endowment. What an organization may liberally call endowment may no more be endowment than are program receipts. Thus, we need to address very carefully the definitions in the law and in the accounting rules. We will do so as an overview here, and then in Chapters 3 and 4 we will go further in depth on each topic.

Endowment as an end use actually comes in three separate forms: 1) true endowment, or donor-restricted, 2) quasi-endowment or funds functioning as endowment (but not really endowment at all) and 3) temporary, or term endowment. True endowment means a donor has expressed intent that the donee not use up the principal, or at least not all of the principal. True endowment is restricted in a written agreement by the donor or is in response to a solicitation that promises to use it in such a restricted way, while quasi-endowment (or funds functioning as endowment, FFE, or board-designated endowment) is designated by board resolution and may be changed by subsequent board resolution. A temporary, or term endowment is meant to be spent over time, but is still donor restricted and, therefore, true endowment.

True endowment is a contract between the donor and the donee. A contract is an agreement between two parties that can arise in different ways. An important term to know is an express contract. An express contract is an agreement *expressly made* between the two parties — for example, between the donor and donee to hold the principal of the transferred funds and spend only the income. There can also be what is called an implied contract where, because of certain actions or due to relying on the promises of another, the first person is bound to carry out the performance of an act. This type of contract may be based on detrimental reliance where one party relies to his or her detriment on what the other party said or did. For instance, the donor may have relied to his or her detriment on your promise that you would hold funds in endowment — in other words, they took action, made a commitment based on a promise you made. You may find detrimental reliance when something has been named in advance of the gift being made. In that case, it is the organization that has relied to its detriment and has taken action or spent money based on a promise or pledge by a donor to make a gift.

There have been cases where a donor has made a promise and a pledge, partially fulfills it and then stops for some reason. The organization is then put to the task of determining whether or not to sue that person for breaking his or her commitment. This concept of implied contract provides all the more reason for endowment policies to be clearly established before funds are raised for endowment.

Another current trend of misunderstanding centers around what is called board-designated endowment. This term is best explained by example. Let's assume a donor leaves in his will an amount that is considered large for an institution, such as $500,000, without any indication that it is restricted as to usage or for endowment. The board decides this would be a nice addition to endowment and votes to add it to endowment. Is this actually endowment?

Assume that the board determines next year that it is in poor financial shape and it needs to use the funds. It votes again, this time to spend the funds. There is no restriction on the board's change of heart. Funds from a board-designated endowment are considered *unrestricted assets*, as opposed to restricted assets. In other words, it is not endowment! Countless organizations think they have endowment when the board sets up a quasi-endowment fund. They do not. They merely have a savings account.

Endowment has a centuries-long legal definition from case law beginning in England hundreds of years ago and continuing to the present time when we have both case law in the U.S. courts as well as more recent legislation. This relatively new legislation (1973–74) is contained in the Uniform Management of Institutional Funds Act. Each state decides whether or not to adopt this legislation, and each state may call it something different. The state may adopt this model legislation in whole or in part.

The legal definition from case law is that funds held as endowment when restricted by donor designation are held in public trust. Thus, the organization's board should explicitly accept this fiduciary responsibility by passing a board resolution. The board should also have a training session as to its legal liability for not following a donor's restriction once it has promised to do so.

The accounting definition requires that the endowment funds be kept separately from all other funds of the entity and the true endowment be separately accounted for and not mingled into quasi-endowment, or FFE (funds functioning as endowment). These are two different types of funds and, legally speaking, funds functioning as endowment are really not legal endowment funds. The courts will not give them protection as to their restrictions as they do for donor-restricted endowments.

In determining how to direct gifts from the various sources into endowment, we must look back at the Development Function Revenue. Which of the funds in the sources of revenue would you want to direct into endowment as opposed to capital or operational? Is there any reason you would want to put any annual operating funds into endowment, or some portion of annual gifts into endowment?

Some organizations promote the endowment of an annual gift, let's say $1,000. What amount of principal would be required to generate conveniently and easily $1,000 a year? From there, you can work backwards into an amount the investment yield from which will result in the yearly amount ($1,000). To do this, you will need to set another assumption to determine what percent yield you are working with. What fund will produce $1,000 per year, say at 5% yield? A $20,000 fund at 5% will generate $1,000, so the gift requested would need to be $20,000 to endow the annual gift.

But generally, it is major gift revenue that is directed into endowment. Of major gift revenue, it does not matter what form the gift takes — outright, in trust or by will. To make a major gift end up as endowment, it requires a restriction by a donor. Where that restriction will be found, however, does depend upon the form. It will generally be in a donor agreement for the lifetime outright gift, in the trust instrument for a trust gift and in the will for a bequest of endowed funds.

Funds from corporate and foundation grants are not likely to be directed into endowment, and funds raised from special appeals and special event giving are not usually destined for endowment. Thus, for the most part, the source of funds for endowment comes from a good, strong major and planned gift program. However, to have that good, strong program, the development needs to know very well how the funds are intended to be *spent* — the end of them. That's what markets the endowment fund. See the section below in this chapter on setting the purpose of the fund. Setting a well-defined purpose can be the fundraiser's best ally.

Restrictions as to Usage

While the donor's restriction to hold the funds as true endowment form one layer of restriction, another layer may be formed on top of that. The donor may say that the spendable income or other distributable amount may only be used for a specific program. If the donor does not further restrict the income of the fund, the income may be used for general purposes. If the donor gives to a fund, the purpose of which is already established, and that purpose is to spend the income in a particular manner, then the income from the donor's transferred funds are presumed to be spent in the same manner for which the endowment fund was created. For example, if the donor contributes to the scholarship endowment, it is assumed that not only is the principal held to generate yield where the principal is unspent, but also the income is to be spent for scholarships. This forms two types of restrictions.

Policies and Guidelines

As you see so far, an endowment has many operational aspects. It is not something that the organization imposes upon itself and it is more than the "rainy day fund" that so many of our clients talk to us about. And it does not hold assets that are used directly in the charitable program. These are very special assets that have legal and accounting rules applicable to them that must be followed to the tee for legal compliance and for a clean audit. Therefore, the organization must develop policies and guidelines to ensure that such funds are properly handled and adequately accounted for. The next several chapters will elaborate on these aspects of setting up your endowment funds.

There are major decisions to be made before policies can be written. We urge you not to borrow and copy policies from one or more other organizations. We believe that every organization is a snowflake and no two are alike. The policies of one do not fit the other. You won't know that until a crisis hits. Then you will know it very well. You need to work with the board, management and key staff to determine what the current thinking is on several issues. Then you must realize that policies are a process, not an event. By this we mean that they will of necessity evolve with time and events. What is a charity other than its current board, officers, management, personnel, members and constituency? We know that changes happen, sometimes slowly and sometimes abruptly. Your decisions and policies will, too. It is essential that you write them out, because if you do not, no one will really know them and no one will own up to them in a time of crisis. In fact, if you just copy those of another organization, you will find yourself in a crisis when the board or management wants to know "what is our policy on this?" They may well ask, "Just who created that policy?"

Commitment to having good policies and guidelines in place starts in writing. So does serious thinking about issues that may crop up. It is better that the organization try to think through difficult issues during calm moments rather than in the middle of a problem matter. Thinking it through during a crisis leads to snap decisions and ones made specifically for the immediate situation. During a problem, the organization may not be thinking well. This is when policies and guidelines serve you best.

Five Parts to the Process of Creating an Endowment Fund

What do these policies contain? Many organizations have policies for legal and accounting questions. Endowment policies are narrower and relate solely to the creation and operation of endowment funds. We have broken down the steps of creating an endowment fund into five parts. Each of these *must precede* the next step to effectively build a well-thought-through fund. The written expression of the intent and implementation of these thoughts is the embodiment of the endowment policy or that which the organization promises to the donor it will do with the contributed funds. The following will introduce the five steps of creating a fund and the thinking process that is necessary to that creation.

These five steps are:

1. Determine the purpose for which the organization will hold an endowment.
2. From this stated purpose, develop a board resolution.
3. From the purpose, set an investment objective that can attain the income or growth necessary to achieve that purpose.
4. From the investment objective and actual investment performance, establish a spending rule, including both distribution for program as well as charges against the fund, if any, for administrative expenses.
5. Create documentation that governs the fund.

Purpose

What is, after all, an endowment fund? Organizations we have worked with at the outset of creating endowment funds often view an endowment fund as a rainy day fund. But that is not the purpose; for that purpose, the organization may as well have a savings account. On that note, remember that a board-designated endowment is, in essence a big savings account and nothing more. Only the donor restricts the usage to endowment, there is no other way to create endowment.

In a consulting situation, one of the authors was asked to make the quasi-endowment irrevocable. Her response was that it was impossible. The board, however, said that it chose to make a certain amount of the organization's yearly surplus irrevocably transfer into an endowment fund and that the board would be the restricting donor. After discussion with other attorneys and endowment consultants, it was concluded that the board would be doing the equivalent of giving to itself. It would be like you, the reader saying, "I hereby make myself a gift and it is irrevocably not to be spent." It is a legal impossibility. You get to change your mind. So does the board placing the restriction or any later board.

Also, endowment assets are assets not functioning in the charitable program of the organization. They are investment assets that are stashed away and restricted as to their usage on a temporary (for a set term) or permanent basis. They are held aside to achieve some goal that lasts for more than the current generation. This leads us directly to consider what that goal is and how it affects setting the purpose of the fund.

What, then, might be the goal of the donor in creating endowment? Centuries ago, before the advent of charities in corporate form, it was a donor who created a trust, the terms of which indicated to the trustee (or trustees) that principal was to be held and invested and the fruit therefrom, the income in the form of interest, dividends, rents and royalties, to be expended for the purposes stated in the trust's governing instrument. Thus, the donor actually established his own endowment. So is it now where a donor establishes a private foundation.

However, with the advent of charities being incorporated during the twentieth century, endowment funds became a part of the assets of the charity accounted for separately. This led to the *charity* determining what it wished to fund in perpetuity, something that related to its overall mission, but perhaps only one aspect of it. This flipped the roles from donor-driven creation of endowment purpose to donee-driven creation of purpose. Thereafter, the donee charity must attract one or more donors to the fund. If the gift is large enough, the charity may work with a donor to create and entirely separate fund rather than including his or her gift in an ongoing fund.

NACUBO has studied the most common purposes for which donee charities have established their endowments. The following embodies those listed purposes, with the authors' comments on their perceptions in relation to these purposes. NACUBO lists them as follows:

1. Perpetual financial independence.
2. Changes in priorities of the organization and its environment
3. Enhance existing programs by supporting their current needs.
4. Expansion of new programs and growth of the organization.
5. Weather unforeseen shortfalls and short-term stresses.
6. Acquisition, improvement, replacement and ongoing maintenance of facilities.
7. Replace an income stream that is drying up.
8. Support a particular program

Let's look at each of these purposes separately. Obviously, there may well be others that pertain to a specific organization and a specific program of that charity.

Perpetual Financial Independence

From the board's point of view, the most likely reason to have endowment is to provide for the long-term health of the organization. Every year in the budgetary process, the board struggles (in most organizations) to make ends meet, to provide the services it stands for and to enhance its programs for the future. These are volunteer board members who are currently serving;

they are representatives of this generation. They are trying to fulfill the duty of a director or trustee to make this organization work, not only on their shift, but for the future as well. They need to find a financial way to perpetuate the services. They have heard about endowment, but they may not know quite what it is or how to get it. But they know it is what *they* want and *you* are supposed to get it.

This motive for starting an endowment can be the most troublesome because the board is obviously not yet educated about endowments and has unrealistic expectations. They will water down the purpose until it is unmarketable; the fundraiser has little sizzle to sell. This is the same board that does not want to adopt a spending rule or an investment objective without knowing what the other organizations are doing fortunately, boards learn and organizations grow.

General endowment may be good or advisable. Large institutions have general endowment funds. Small ones or young ones often see this as the rainy day account, and many do not realize they cannot tap into it for the rainy day. This very thing had gotten some boards fined by the attorney general of their state. Principal of an endowment fund is sacred. It is restricted in accordance with the laws of the state and the donor agreement. It may not be invaded for the rainstorm.

Perpetual financial independence that is intended to substitute for good, recurring fundraising is also not acceptable. We have come across too many organizations that are not capable of achieving a flow of annual gifts sufficient to support the organization, and therefore believe they will eliminate the need for fundraising by having an endowment. If an organization cannot convince a donor to give a small amount annually, how in the world can it convince several to give large amounts for the future?

So is perpetual financial independence a good goal? Of course, but it may not be the most marketable as an endowment program. A better-defined, more concrete and alluring goal may bring in more gifts and ease the pressure on current operational funds to support future needs, allowing the organization to focus on using current money for current programs and specially raised endowment for future needs.

Changes in Priorities of the Organization and Its Environment

It's amazing how we sometimes forget that life twists and turns of its own accord. That is true for individuals as well as organizations. Needs change, emergencies happen, society evolves, new discoveries alter lives of constituents, all of which requires a different or redefined focus of the organization purporting to serve the public.

While the organization is busy making ends meet to carry out its purpose on a daily basis, how will it respond to shifts in priorities, whether they come like earthquakes or whether they move in like the change of a season? Too often the organization is struggling to maintain its work daily and does look at changing needs, if they are foreseeable at all, in advance. One good purpose for a special purpose endowment fund is to meet the changing needs of the organization. As opposed to the question of what to do with, for example, money donated to cancer research when the cure has been found (there are many other diseases), the question here is, what if we find an *additional, new, unforeseen* need that falls within our charter? Will we be able to step in and address it? Yes, with this type of endowment.

Enhance Existing Programs by Supporting Their Current Needs

As opposed to finding a substutute for the need for annual fundraising, what if an organization in fact knew that an endowment could be created to fund a specific purpose; it could turn its focus to immediate fundraising needs and program expenditures for other purposes that donors might be less inclined to endow.

Support of a current effort through endowment in some part, or in large part, serves to take the pressure off that one and permits other activities to be the current focus. You may analogize it to paying the expenses of a rental property from the income of the property so you can save for or pay for children's education from current wages. One type of charitable program may be better suited to marketing for endowment gifts than another.

A small private college sent a brochure, actually a very clever marketing brochure, to its alumni, with a picture of pens and paperclips and chairs and phones and desks and the like. No text appeared on the front. Inside it said, "No one wants to endow these things, but we need them every day." It was done in a very appealing way and was open and honest. And most of all, it was true.

Expansion of New Programs and Growth of the Organization

Planning in advance for new programs is quite different than enhancing existing programs. Whether simply new endeavors or the growing operations of the organization as a whole, this type of fund is one of the most exciting for donors. Who doesn't want to fund something new and exciting?

New programs are exciting and marketable. If this purpose fits, it sells, whether it's a new wing of a hospital, a new school for a university, new programming for public television or new scientific research. It generally attracts gifts to endowment.

Weather Unforeseen Shortfalls and Short-Term Stresses

An endowment fund can also serve to weather unforeseen shortfalls and short-term stresses that occur as a result of liabilities, whether legal or media related. Here's an example. An organization had a disgruntled employee leave on a less than favorable basis. He then went to the Attorney General, claiming the management, from the Executive Director through the Vice President and Director of Development were spending organizational money for personal use, contending basically that they were embezzling funds. It hit the newspapers that the Director of Development had a $6,000 a year travel and expense budget to talk to donors.

For an active development effort with constituents in various states, that may have in fact been too meager, but in the papers it looked awful. The constituents — it was a true charity supporting constituents — were out in the streets picketing, making a public scene with media coverage of all types, radio, television and newspapers. It was horrible for the organization. In fact, the Attorney General stepped in but found that the Vice President had been in Italy on a personal trip, and although everything was personally paid for, he inadvertently bought a $121 pair of shoes on his business credit card. When he returned, he repaid it promptly. Many people use the wrong card by mistake and correct it as soon as they realize it. Is this embezzlement of organizational funds? Well, all of it was a tempest in a teapot and the Attorney General found really nothing improper, but what happened to the fundraising of that organization? It was down to zero for several years. They had a long fight to get their image back. This is one illustration where a healthy endowment fund would help weather unforeseen short-term liabilities.

Acquisition, Improvement, Replacement and Ongoing Maintenance of Facilities

This may be one of the more popular types of endowment purpose. Although the NACUBO study did not give percentages or numbers of organizations that used these purposes, certainly, most organizations today will, in a capital campaign, have an endowment element. The campaign is for building, improving or buying capital assets, such as facilities for the organization. The current funds raised for the capital are generally spent on that acquisition. The endowment portion of such a fundraising effort is designed to provide funds for the future maintenance and operation of the facilities. Capital campaigns are more tangible than many other end uses of funds from the donor's point of view. They know exactly what the organization intends to do with their money. They know what their dollars will buy. So, too, with the endowment portion of such a campaign. From a marketing perspective, it is one of the easier ways to fund an endowment.

Replace an Income Stream that Is Drying Up

Many young organizations raise funds from special events. At some point they grow up and realize that this is the highest cost of fundraising and therefore the lowest return on the dollar. The organization becomes aware that it must expand its fundraising effort into all areas of fundraising, including the major gift area. It takes time to build the relationships that result in major gifts. If they think it through, they will also realize that a day will come when the special events will cap out at a certain level of income. It is at this point that organizations often determine they had better start looking at ensuring their future with another way to derive income.

For example, a membership organization with chapters nationwide supported itself for years on chapter banquets. After many years the increase in banquet revenue began to fall off while expenditures to operate the organization continued to increase. The organization began two specific purpose endowment funds to ease the pressure.

It may be that an organization provides services that are changing with societal needs, leading it to require the stability of endowment income. In any event, a well-planned endowment fund can replace this source of income.

Support a Particular Program

One of the most popular types of endowments is to fund a specific program well known to donors or well liked by donors. For example, support for a professorship, or scholarships, or an art program, or for programming for public broadcasting or the many, many special purpose endowments that organizations of all types have. The donor knows exactly what he or she is buying with his or her dollars. If there is true interest in the purpose, this fund will succeed.

Selecting Your Purpose

As to the specific purpose for your endowment fund, first you must ask, "Will it support the basic mission of the organization?" No endowment fund for which you seek money can possibly exist and succeed if the donors view it as contrary to the general purposes for which the organization exists. Even if it is not contrary, it must enhance the mission. It must be a positive.

So what will be the specific reason for creating a particular endowment fund? Here is an exercise that will help you form a mission statement just for the endowment fund in question. Finish this sentence: "We are creating this endowment fund because…" Then finish the second sentence: "It will provide our organization with (help us achieve)…"

Each of these statements must be completed in one sentence, no more, not in a little paragraph or any other material. It must be succinct, meaningful and carry your message and not be vague! This will form the mission statement, or purpose for this endowment fund. Most importantly, when you're ready to seek funding, you must appeal to the donor. You must be clear, specific and somehow pull at the heartstrings, let them know what a difference this *gift* will make.

There are two theories to examine in considering this exercise of stating your purpose. One is product orientation and the other is consumer orientation. Product orientation focuses on the product, such as a car. Consumer orientation focuses on what that car will do for the consumer. Keep these in mind when you work on your purpose.

Resolution

This stated purpose is the basis for the board resolution. Drafting a board resolution, in fact, is quite simple once you have answered the above questions and taken the necessary steps. Be sure, however, that your stated purpose is also a goal of the board. As you probably do with any resolution that you put forward, circulate it for comment but be prepared to defend it exactly as written or as closely thereto as possible.

In terms of the actual writing, keep it away from the lawyers and the committees. Committee writings have a tendency to become more and more vague as they are worked on because few people in an organizational setting will commit to specific things. Vagueness suits group thinking and low-level achievement. Boldness and innovation requires precision, but not necessarily perfection. Warren Buffet has been quoted as saying that he would rather be approximately right than precisely wrong.

You will find a sample board resolution in Appendix C. Although it is short, it is highly important to state exactly what the organization wants in a fund. This resolution will make the rest of the job either easy or maddening. The more it is watered down, the less it says and therefore the less guidance fundraisers, investment managers, business office and donors have.

Investment Objective

To form an appropriate investment objective, one must look at the stated purpose (see above) that the organization intends to accomplish with this particular endowment fund. First, the organization must determine whether the stated purpose requires more current income or more growth for the future. Take a look at two of the stated purposes above. One is to enhance and support existing programs. Obviously, that will require that income be spent now on projects. On the other hand, to provide for expansion and growth of future programs will not require a current income flow, but will require growing funds to meet future needs.

You can readily see that the current income fund requires a certain type of investment, heavier in income production, and the other can afford to have more in long-term growth with little or no current income generation. The investment managers absolutely need this guidance if the organization believes it will carry out the purpose of this fund.

A related question is whether the organization hopes to achieve generational neutrality to ensure that this generation gets no more and no fewer benefits than subsequent generations. In other words, is the purpose of this fund slanted to more current or more deferred benefits? These questions, or the answers to them that your organization develops, will set your investment objective without the typical noncommittal board question, "Well, what are other organizations doing?" Who cares? *Their* needs and their funds and their programs are entirely different. *Their* investments therefore will not achieve *your* stated goal.

Spending Policy

The organization must determine three parts of the spending policy. First, what will be the spending *rule*, or on what basis will funds be spent. Then, what spending *rate* does this produce regularly to meet the needs of the program. Third, what *fees* may be assessed against the income or amount to be distributed for program purposes?

The spending rule will permit the organization to decide whether it will promote gifts the entire principal of which will be held inviolate, or where some or all appreciation, or even some principal, may be spent. It will also permit the organization to determine whether it will decline donor restrictions on spending that do not comply with the organizational decision due to the administrative needs for separate accounting. In the next chapter, the spending rule will be discussed from a legal perspective — what does the state legislature say may be spent, to what degree may the organization vary from this, and to what degree may the donor affect it?

The spending rate must achieve a flow of revenue to support the stated purpose for the usage of that revenue, if any. What spending policy should the board adopt to achieve this every year? Well, that depends on how the fund is invested, which depends on the state purpose of the fund. Thus, you can see that the purpose, the investment objective and the spending policies are all inextricably tied together if the endowment is to work smoothly.

So how does a board determine a policy for what it will spend from the endowment each year? First, it must consider what it said the purpose of the fund is, a more current need, a more deferred need or a desire to spend on a basis that is neutral over the generations, balancing the present with the future, or generational neutrality.

Next, it must consider what the fund earns in a *real* sense. For example, if a portfolio with an asset mix of 60% equities and 40% fixed income earns at a total return of 9%, and the rate of inflation is running about 3%, it has a real rate of return of 6% before expenses (historical real rates of return average about 7% for stocks and 2% for bonds).

It may, as part of its policy, assess an overhead expense of 0.5% against the income of the fund. Thus, its net return is 5.5% before fees of managers. Let's assume management fees are 1.5%. The return available for spending is 4%. Is the budget for the endowed program growing in excess of this rate? Will the state's governing law allow an incursion into real principal (other than accrued but unrealized gain) to keep pace or can the board change either its investment mix or its spending policy? Can it change the budget for the supported program?

Other factors to include in the decision-making process are the financial health this year, the fundraising potential and actual performance, the need for yet new programs, and the current economy.

In a survey of spending policy each year, NACUBO found eight basic spending policies:

1. all current income,
2. pre-specified percentage of current income,
3. pre-specified percentage of market value,
4. pre-specified percentage of moving average,
5. increase last year's spending by specified percent,
6. decide each year,
7. other rule and
8. no established policy.

Looking at numbers six, seven and eight, put yourself in the donor's shoes. If you were going to make a gift of $1 million for the swimming program, and the policy of this organization is that the board will *decide on a yearly basis* what it would like to spend on a swimming program, how marketable is that? A donor who chooses to support the swimming program no doubt wants to be guaranteed that *something* is going to be spent on the swimming program every year. Total board discretion, also means they have total discretion to spend nothing. That is not a good policy for marketing purposes, or even for later donor-relations purposes, yet some organizations choose it.

If we look at spending the income or last year's income plus a percentage it is possibly more predictable for budgeting, but not for asset preservation. Spending based on a percent of value (total return) of this year or a moving average of years is more asset preservation oriented, but less predictable for budgeting.

Keep in mind that for hundreds of years the concept of endowment was to spend all the income, not just a percent times value, but all the income — dividends, interest, rents and royalties. The more recent policies keep things as flexible as possible in an inflexible environment. Endowment is an inflexible environment. In a basically "hold the principal, spend the income" environment, how can we make it more flexible? The bulk of the reporting colleges and universities choose percent times value on a 3–4 year moving average of the fund's values.

The final piece is to determine what the costs may be of operating this fund and whether the organization will bear the costs out of current budget or whether it is more equitable for the fund itself to bear its own costs. This is another form of question about generational neutrality. Should current donors and program fees support the cost of holding an endowment, the income from which will benefit people and programs generations from now?

At an institution where one of the authors once worked, a donor gave $1 million into endowment. The spending rule at the time was a fixed percentage of 5% times the yearly value. The organization determined in its operating guidelines that it would charge a fee for carrying the fund on its books — for doing the work — to cover their overhead. But what if it never told the donor that?

The donor thought the organization would spend 5% on his or her favorite program, but what if the organization subtracts 0.5% for general overhead every year for 25 years, and then the donor discovers it? And, what if it were a bigger endowment gift, say of $20 million instead of $1 million? That money charged for administration starts to rack up. Eventually the donor or the family may come back and say, "You never told us you were going to take that 0.5% every year for 20 years on this fund. That amount plus interest equals $X. Please restore it." How would you like to be in that situation?

It has happened. What would it cost for the organization to take from its general funds an amount sufficient to restore the assessed costs to this person's endowment account? This is precisely why you want a policy established up front that is communicated to donors before the gift is made. One of the worst mistakes we see across the country is not telling donors the policies on endowment, if they have them, and, even worse, is not having policies at all.

Documents

There are three basic parts to the documentation of an endowment fund: 1) policies and guidelines, 2) donor agreements and 3) acceptance procedures. It is important to have each of these worked out and written out before soliciting gifts on a broad-scale basis.

As to the policies and guidelines, all of the above pertaining to the five parts to the process of setting up of the fund should be contained in written form to create the policies and guidelines for the operation of the endowment. These guidelines must include the board and committee decisions made in the section above. This document can also be the basis for marketing and promotional materials.

The donor agreement is the contract with the donor, and if there is none, then the contract is an *implied* contract based on the oral or written representations or promotional material of the organization. A donor or family of the donor may not be able to directly enforce this contract other than through a claim of *detrimental reliance,* but it can have an effect on the execution of the endowment fund by complaint to the Attorney General. A donor who misunderstood or never knew the real relationship or terms of the deal can also cause you great problems with donor relations and media liability.

Acceptance procedures are also important before things slip through the cracks. Every organization must develop its own step-by-step process of taking in an endowment fund gift. There are no set rules here. The staff of each organization needs to walk through a hypothetical gift, every step of the way from the development office and on to the business office, setting the path and procedures along the way. In other words, create a case study before you ever accept a gift. Walking it through the development office and on to the business office and then to the investment manager and on through the receipt of revenue and use for program expenses will expose any area that needs coordination or study. Look at all aspects you can think of: the governing document terms, execution, asset transfer, booking of the asset, setting up the account, selling of the asset, reinvestment of the proceeds and ongoing monitoring of the correct use of the revenue for the purpose stated. This should be set down in writing so all departments know exactly how this endowment is to function in advance.

If you are disciplined enough to have all those documents for every endowment fund, you will not have crises, you will not be sued, you will not have families calling you and asking whether you did this work correctly once the donor turned assets over to you, and other such problems will not arise. See Appendix C for sample documents and agreements.

3

Legal Aspects

Distribution of Income; Retention of Principal

Historically, endowed charitable gifts have been made in trust controlled by the trustee. For centuries this was the case. Donors wrote into the trust instrument the requirement to hold the funds in perpetuity, and in many cases indicating to the trustee how to expend the income. What to spend, the "income," was therefore defined by trust law concepts of what was income and what was principal. Income was generally considered the fruits produced by the asset — rents, royalties, interest and dividends. That held true for hundreds of years until more than halfway through the twentieth century when it became possible to consider gain or growth in value distributable along with income.

Doctrine of *Cy Pres*

In another vein, trust law required that the trustee adhere to the stated purpose. While charitable trusts can last hundreds of years, needs of society change and sometime the stated trust purpose no longer fits charitable needs. As a result of this phenomenon, a doctrine developed called the doctrine of *cy pres*. Actually, the full term was *cy pres comme possible*, or as near as possible. This was used to mollify the effects of the irrevocability of the trust and its stated charitable purpose.

Under the rule of *cy pres*, if a devise to charity is impossible, or impracticable of fulfillment, equity will substitute another charitable object which is believed to approach the original purpose as closely as possible.

The rule of *cy pres* is a rule of legal construction. It will be applied only when the court, construing the terms of a will or other dispositive document, determines that the testator intended to make a charitable disposition regardless of whether the disposition could be carried out in the particular way called for in the will. The rule will be invoked only when the testator is found to have had a "general charitable intent."

A testator is said to have had a "general charitable intent" when the particular disposition is of a generally charitable nature and not intended to benefit a specific charitable entity. On the other hand, if the gift is intended to benefit only a specific beneficiary, the *cy pres* rule cannot be invoked because its application may be contrary to the donor's intent.

The *cy pres* rule has been applied to uphold gifts when the named recipients have refused to accept them, when the recipients could not be identified with certainty, when the donee of a charitable gift did not exist at the date of the decedent's death, when the name of the devisee as set forth in the will ambiguously identified more than one charitable recipient, and when the testator did not specify a precise charitable purpose or name a specific charity as the recipient of a devise.

When the court invokes the *cy pres* rule, it directs that the property be applied to a charitable purpose related the purpose originally intended by the transferor. The court may, for instance, order that the devised property be distributed to a charitable organization that performs the same function as the organization named in the will or, if there is no such organization, to an organization that performs a function that closely matches the function of the original organization. (This section on *cy pres* is taken from *California Will & Trusts*, Chapter 30, "Charitable Devises," by L.S. Moerschbaecher, published by Matthew Bender & Co., Inc.).

The Advent of the Charity as Corporation

When charities became incorporated instead of operating in trust form, debates and issues emerged on several points. For example, should corporations hold what is the equivalent of a trust as endowment and, if so, what is income for the purpose of spending the income of the fund so held if the trust laws of income and principal do not apply to corporations? A trust is a separate legal entity and if a corporation holds funds in trust as endowment (as opposed to just holding the endowment as a fund on the balance sheet and separately accounting for it), does this necessitate, under U.S. federal tax laws, that the organization obtain an exempt status for the trust, or is it a part of the nonprofit corporation's exemption? If it is part of the exemption of the corporation should it be held as a fund that is not legally a trust? If it is not a trust, but a corporate fund, can it be held in perpetuity and can the restricted use be enforced?

These are some of the issues that surfaced in the twentieth century as the number of charities created in corporate form grew by leaps and bounds. Until the last twenty years of the century, many states did not have statutes that pertained specifically to nonprofit corporations. If they did have nonprofit corporation laws, they were often simply a part of the general business corporation law. In the last twenty years of the century, the model Nonprofit Corporations Act was drafted and adopted by many states.

In addition, in response to some of the management issues raised in practice with nonprofits, the Uniform Management of Institutional Funds Act (UMIFA) was also drafted and adopted in many states. In cases where a state adopts the model or uniform law, each state has the right to select or reject provisions, to modify those provisions or to adopt the law in whole. Therefore, every organization must check its own state law to learn the nonprofit corporate code or UMIFA rules adopted by that particular state.

These corporate laws, especially the UMIFA, responded to some far-sighted (and maybe also some short-sighted) thinkers. In the article cited above, Brody reported a portion of the letter of gift to the trustees of the John Solomon Guggenheim Memorial Foundation:

> No one can foresee the future, and limitations which seem wise today might become impracticable or injurious in later years. No man of wisdom would seek perpetually to bind you and your successors to fixed plans and methods involving fixed studies, causes, places or institutions...Yet it seems to me appropriate that I should indicate to you those general purposes and policies, within the scope of the charter, to which I wish you and your successors to conform as long as is deemed best. If, at some distant time, it seems wisest in the careful judgment of the Trustees, to change or disregard them, you have here a statement of my wish that you do so; you will conform best to my wishes by using your own good judgment.

Trust law had little or no flexibility to allow for change of purpose. The UMIFA has that as one of its most important features. Many other features of the UMIFA have permitted flexibility. Not all states have adopted the UMIFA, and not all states have adopted it in the form of the model act, but have made changes according to the desires of that state's legislature.

A Closer Look at the UMIFA

The Adoption of the Act

The National Conference of Commissioners on Uniform State Laws prepared, through one of its committees, the Uniform Management of Institutional Funds Act (UMIFA). It was presented in 1972 at the Annual Conference of the Commissioners. The final acts and the pending drafts are publicly available either through The National Conference of Commissioners on Uniform State Laws, 1155 East Sixtieth Street, Chicago, Illinois 60637, or its website, *www.nccusl.org*.

The prefatory notes tell the story of why this act was drafted and then adopted by so many states. It is included here in its entirety:

PREFATORY NOTE

Over the past several years the governing boards of eleemosynary institutions, particularly colleges and universities, have sought to make more effective use of endowment and other investment funds. They and their counsel have wrestled with questions as to permissible investments, delegation of investment authority, and use of the total return concept in investing endowment funds. Studies of the legal authority and responsibility for the management of the funds of an institution have pointed up the uncertain state of the law in most jurisdictions. There is virtually no statutory law regarding trustees or governing boards of eleemosynary institutions, and case law is sparse. In the late 1960's the Ford Foundation commissioned Professor William L. Cary and Craig B. Bright, Esq. to examine the legal restrictions on the powers of trustees and managers of colleges and universities to invest endowment funds to achieve growth, to maintain purchasing power, and to expend a prudent portion of appreciation in endowment funds. They concluded that there was little developed law but that legal impediments which have been thought to deprive managers of their freedom of action appear on analysis to be more legendary than real. Cary and Bright, *The Law and the Lore of Endowment Funds*, 66 (1969).

Nonetheless it appears that counsel for some colleges and universities have advised to the contrary, basing such advice upon analogy to the law of private trusts. Not all counsel, of course, suggest that private trust laws control the governing boards of eleemosynary institutions.

There is, however, substantial concern about the potential liability of the managers of the institutional funds even though cases of actual liability are virtually nil. As deliberations of the Special Committee, the Advisory Committee and the Reporters responsible for the preparation of this Act have progressed, it became clear that the problems were not unique to educational institutions but were faced by any charitable, religious or any other eleemosynary institution which owned a fund to be invested.

One further problem regularly intruded upon the discussion of efforts to free trustees and managers from the alleged limitations on their powers to invest for growth and meet the financial needs of their institutions. Some gifts and grants contained restrictions on use of funds or selection of investments which imperiled the effective management of the fund. An expeditious means to modify obsolete restrictions seemed necessary.

The Uniform Act offers a rational solution to these problems by providing:

(1) a standard of prudent use of appreciation in invested funds;

(2) specific investment authority;

(3) authority to delegate investment decisions;

(4) a standard of business care and prudence to guide governing boards in the exercise of their duties under the Act; and

(5) a method of releasing restrictions on use of funds or selection of investments by donor acquiescence or court action.

Use of Appreciation

The argument for allowing prudent use of appreciation of endowment funds has been stated in Cary and Bright, *The Law and the Lore of Endowment Funds* 5–6 (1969):

[T]oo often the desperate need of some institutions for funds to meet current operating expenses has led their managers, contrary to their best long-term judgment, to forego investments with favorable growth prospects if they have a low current yield.

[I]t would be far wiser to take capital gains as well as dividends and interest into account in investing for the highest overall return consistent with the safety and preservation of the funds invested. If the current return is insufficient for the institution's needs, the difference between that return and what it would have been under a more restrictive policy can be made up by the use of a prudent portion of capital gains.

The Uniform Act authorizes expenditure of appreciation subject to a standard of business care and prudence. It seems unwise to fix more exact standards in a statute. To impose a greater construction would hamper adaption by different institutions to their particular needs.

The standard of care is that of a reasonable and prudent director of a nonprofit corporation — similar to that of a director of a business corporation — which seems more appropriate than the traditional Prudent Man Rule applicable to private trustees. The approach has been used elsewhere. A New York statute allows inclusion in income of "so much of the realized appreciation as the board may deem prudent." New York Not-for-Profit Corporation Law § 513(d) (1970). Recent enactments in New Jersey, California, and Rhode Island follow the same pattern. N.J.S.A. § 15:18-8; West's Anno. Corp. Code § 10251(c) (Calif.); Gen. Laws of R.I. § 18-12-2.

The Act authorizes the appropriation of net appreciation. "Realization" of gains and losses is an artificial, meaningless concept in the context of a nontaxable eleemosynary institution. If gains and losses had to be realized before being taken into account, a major objective of the Act, to avoid distortion of sound investment policies, would be frustrated. If only realized capital gains could be taken into account, trustees or managers might be forced to sell their best assets, appreciated property, in order to produce spendable gains and conceivably might spend realized gains even when, because of unrealized losses, the fund has no net appreciation.

The Act excludes interests held for private beneficiaries, even though a charity is the ultimate beneficiary, e.g., an individual life interest followed by a charitable reminder. Also excluded is any trust managed by a professional trustee even though a charitable organization is the sole beneficiary.

The Uniform Act has been drafted to meet the objection that there will be a decline in gifts to charity because donors cannot rely on their wishes being enforced if appreciation can be expended. The drafters were convinced that donors seldom give any indication of how they want the growth in their gifts to be treated. If, however, a donor does indicate that he wishes to limit expenditures to ordinary yield, under the Act his wishes will be respected.

A statute such as this can be constitutionally applied to gifts received prior to its enactment. There is no substantial authority to be found in law or reason for denying retroactive application.

When the Uniform Principal and Income Act was adopted it changed the apportionment of some items of revenue between principal and income. It was argued that the retroactive application of the statute to existing trusts would deprive either the income beneficiaries or the remaindermen of the property without due process of law. Professor Scott spoke for the overwhelming majority of commentators when he said:

[T]here should be no constitutional objection to making the Act retroactive. The rules as to allocation should not be treated as absolute rules of property law, but rather as rules as to the administration of the trust. The purpose is to make allocations which are fair and impartial as between the successive beneficiaries. Scott, *Principal or Income?, 100 Trusts & Est.* 180, 251 (1961).

Professor Bogert reached the same conclusion. Bogert, *The Law of Trusts and Trustees* § 847, pp. 505–6 (2d ed. 1962). The courts which considered the matter reached the same conclusion.

There is even less reason to deny retroactive application to an apportionment statute which deals only with the endowment funds of eleemosynary institutions, because the statute does not deprive any beneficiary of vested property rights. In a broad sense, the public is the real beneficiary of an endowment fund. The only argument which can be made against retroactivity is that it might violate the intent of the donor. Such an argument was also made in respect of the Uniform Principal and Income Act, but it was uniformly rejected by the courts. The language of a Minnesota case is typical:

[I]t is doubtful whether testatrix had any clear intention in mind at the time the will was executed. It is equally plausible that if she had thought about it at all she would have desired to have the dividends go where the law required them to go at the time they were received by the trustee...*In re Gardner's Trust*, 266 Minn. 127, 132, 123 N.W. 2d 69, 73 (1963).

In any event, the Act does not raise a problem of retroactive application because the rule of construction of Section 3 is declaratory of existing law in that it interprets the presumed intent of the donor in the absence of a clear statement of the donor's intention.

Other similar acts follow the same pattern. The New York Not-for-Profit Corporation Law Section 513(e) (1970) authorizing the expenditure of appreciation applies to assets "held at the time when this chapter takes effect" as well as to "assets hereafter received." Similar language appears in the New Jersey, California, and Rhode Island acts authorizing expenditure of appreciation by eleemosynary institutions.

Specific Investment Authority

It seems reasonably clear that investment managers of endowment funds are not limited to investments authorized to trustees. The broad grant of investment authority contained in Section 4 of the Act expressly so provides.

Authority to Delegate

In the absence of clear law relating to the powers of governing boards of eleemosynary institutions, some boards have been advised that they are subject to the nondelegation strictures of professional private trustees. The board of an eleemosynary institution should be able to delegate day-to-day investment management to committees or employees and to purchase investment advisory or management services. The Act so provides.

Standard of Care

Fear of liability of a private trustee may have a debilitating effect upon members of a government board, who are often uncompensated public-spirited citizens. They are managers of nonprofit corporations, guiding a unique and perhaps very large institution. The proper standard of responsibility is more analogous to that of a director of a business corporation than that of a professional private trustee. The Act establishes a standard of business care and prudence in the context of the operation of a nonprofit institution.

Release of Restrictions

It is established law that the donor may place restrictions on his largesse which the donee institution must honor. Too often, the restrictions on use or investment become outmoded or wasteful or unworkable. There is a need for review of obsolete restrictions and a way of modifying or adjusting them. The Act authorizes the governing board to obtain the acquiescence of the donor to a release of restrictions and, in the absence of the donor, to petition the appropriate court for relief in appropriate cases.

Conclusion

Over a decade ago, Professor Kenneth Karst in an article in the *Harvard Law Review* stated the need for the Uniform Act:

[T]he managers of corporate charity are still, at this late date, without adequate guides for conduct. The development of these standards is of some urgency. "The Efficiency of the Charitable Dollar: An Unfilled State Responsibility," 73 *Harv. L. Rev.* 433, 435 (1960).

Working with Certain Provisions Thirty Years Later

It is important that every business office managing endowment funds have a copy of its own state's version of the UMIFA to refer to when questions arise. In this section, we will examine certain provisions using the model act version so the administrator can understand the flow of the legal terminology and the statutory scheme.

Beginning with section one of the act, the terms must be understood. The following text is arranged so that a section of the act appears first, followed by comments on it in italics from the point of view of both the development office and the business office. The Commissioners' comments in the previous section were made in 1972. Much has happened in the development world since then, including the explosion of planned giving and the advent of development of endowment funds via deferred split gift vehicles.

UNIFORM MANAGEMENT OF INSTITUTIONAL FUNDS ACT

1.   Definitions

In this Act

(1) "Institution" means an incorporated or unincorporated organization organized and operated exclusively for educational, religious, charitable, or other eleemosynary purposes, or a governmental organization to the extent that it holds funds exclusively for any of these purposes;

The definition of institution includes both nonprofit corporations and wholly charitable trusts, i.e., those trusts all of the income and principal of which are irrevocably dedicated to charitable purposes. This excludes such things as charitable remainder trusts and pooled income funds because those vehicles do not hold funds exclusively for educational, religious, charitable or other eleemosynary purposes.

(2) "Institutional fund" means a fund held by an institution for its exclusive use, benefit, or purposes, but does not include (i) a fund held for an institution by a trustee that is not an institution or (ii) a fund in which a beneficiary that is not an institution has an interest, other than possible rights that could arise upon violation or failure of the purposes of the fund;

Note that an institutional fund is held for the institution's exclusive benefit. Specifically excluded are "funds held for an institution by a trustee that is not an institution." That means, for example, if a bank or trust company holds a trust that is wholly charitable, all income is to be paid and principal to be held and dedicated for LMNOP charity. This fund, even though exclusively for LMNOP's charitable uses, is not an institutional fund because the trustee holding the funds is not itself an "institution" by definition in section (1) above.

Secondly, excluded are funds where there is a beneficiary that is not an institution, such as a charitable remainder trust that pays an individual.

(3) "Endowment fund" means an institutional fund, or any part thereof, not wholly expendable by the institution on a current basis under the terms of the applicable gift instrument;

Note that the definition of endowment fund does not say that all of the principal must remain inviolate. It says a fund that is not entirely spendable by the institution (some principal must remain intact) and it says this must be the case as a result of the applicable gift instrument. In other words, it must be donor restricted in order to be endowment. Board designated endowment does not count in this definition. That is not held under terms of a gift instrument, but rather by corporate resolution of the governing board.

(4) "Governing board" means the body responsible for the management of an institution or of an institutional fund;

What is the body responsible for the management of an institutional fund? Might that include an investment committee that has formal delegation from the corporate board?

(5) "Historic dollar value" means the aggregate fair value in dollars of (i) an endowment fund at the time it became an endowment fund, (ii) each subsequent donation to the fund at the time it is made, and (iii) each accumulation made pursuant to a direction in the applicable gift instrument at the time the accumulation is added to the fund. The determination of historic dollar value made in good faith by the institution is conclusive.

Looking at the first subsection, when does a fund become an endowment fund exactly? For example, if a donor signs a gift agreement and transfers money, the fund comes into existence. However, if the same donor signs a charitable remainder trust and transfers money, and in that trust, states that at the end of the beneficiary's life this money will be endowment, is the historic dollar value of that endowment the amount when the trust is created or when the beneficiary dies? The fund cannot be endowment under section (3) above until it is an institutional *fund. Funds in a charitable remainder trust are not institutional funds because there is an outstanding non-institutional beneficiary (not exclusively for the use of the institution). Thus, the historic dollar value will be as of the date of the termination of the charitable remainder trust.*

The next two subsections are not complicated. Additions become endowment when received into the fund. Further, if a donor requires in the gift agreement that some accumulated amount be added to the fund, whether that comes from accumulated income in the form of interest, dividends, rents or royalties, or from gain on principal, that becomes endowment when the gift agreement says it is to be added and, in fact, is added to the endowment fund.

(6) "Gift instrument" means a will, deed, grant, conveyance, agreement, memorandum, writing, or other governing document (including the terms of any institutional solicitations from which an institutional fund resulted) under which property is transferred to or held by an institution as an institutional fund.

The definition of gift instrument starts out rather bland, but becomes more interesting as it includes two very fascinating terms. First, the word writing is so very broad. For example, if a development officer is sitting with a donor having a cocktail and the donor writes a check for a million dollars and then writes on the cocktail napkin that this amount is to endow a program, that, in fact, is the gift instrument. If the development officer has the authority to accept such gifts and takes the gift, the institution is bound to follow the gift agreement.

Even more interesting is the parenthetical. What is "any institutional solicitation" in the same context? Let's say the donor called the development officer and said, "I received your brochure on endowment gifts and would like to meet with you about my contribution to the endowment fund." Then the two meet for the cocktail and at the end of the meeting the donor hands the development officer a check. This money was most likely given as a direct result of the institutional solicitation *and is now endowment. But what if there were no such mailing and it was only a solicitation orally made by the development officer who was meeting with the donor as part of his or her job, not a personal social event, and the officer asked the donor to contribute to the endowment fund. Then when the CFO sees the $1,000,000 with no other applicable gift agreement to be found, wants to use the money for operating expenses. Is it endowment or is it operational budget and wholly expendable? This subsection is so broad that, provided the development officer was acting in the scope of his employment, such solicitation would likely fall into the term "any institutional solicitation."*

The moral of the story here is that what one ordinarily thinks of when the term gift agreement or gift instrument is used is simply one of the ways endowment can be created by the donor. Caution is advised in solicitations.

2.   Appropriation of Appreciation

The governing board may appropriate for expenditure for the uses and purposes for which an endowment fund is established so much of the net appreciation, realized and unrealized, in the fair value of the assets of an endowment fund over the historic dollar value of the fund as is prudent under the standard established by Section 6. This Section does not limit the authority of the governing board to expend funds as permitted under other law, the terms of the applicable gift instrument, or the charter of the institution.

We need to look at four elements of this little but powerful provision — first, net appreciation, realized and unrealized; second, prudent standard; third, expenditures only for the uses for which the fund is established; and fourth, the authority of the board.

Net appreciation means net gains over losses, but what is not addressed here is the time period over which the netting occurs. Is it yearly, or is it possible cumulatively? The Commissioners state that the concept of realization (that is to say, the sale or disposition of the asset so that the gain is experienced) is meaningless in the context of a nontaxable institution. Is that true? Only if the subject of discussion is taxation. Without a concept of realization, how do we come to what is net as opposed to gross because net means, on some time frame, subtracting the losses from the gains. This could be done on a yearly or other discrete time basis without realization, but if no time frame is included, it is instead simply a cumulative recordkeeping of historic versus total value. Then it is really a gross concept, not a net concept. The way this is written is more amenable to a snapshot in time in gross valuation, which forms the base for the spending rate and frequency. Then, according to the donor's restriction, some or all of the historic dollar value may not be spent. The balance may be, however, subject to the prudent person standard found later in the act. The point on realization is well-founded, however, in that if realization were the standard, the managers would have to sell off their best assets to use for expenditures, leaving them the dogs. The provision just leaves the netting concept unfinished.

The prudent standard adopted in a later section is intended to make this more like a business corporation standard than a trust standard.

Third, when capital appreciation is in fact used, it must be used for the same purpose as in the gift agreement. If the fund earns much more than imagined, perhaps the donor, while alive, could release the restriction by amending the agreement in accordance with the written release provision in a later section.

Last, the authority of the board to spend appreciation is limited to what is permitted under other law, the terms of the applicable gift instrument, or the charter of the institution. If the state has passed other law, that law may limit the board's discretion. Clearly, the donor can override this expenditure in the gift instrument, but if the donor's gift agreement is too difficult to administer, the organization does not have to accept the gift. What is meant by the charter of the organization is not clear. Does that mean only the Articles of Incorporation? In many states today, those are slim, boilerplate documents giving no specific powers. It would seem to include the bylaws, too, but perhaps not resolutions and guidelines approved by the board. It might be helpful to make a reference in the bylaws that the passage of endowment policies by the board is required, and then to have those guidelines approved by resolution. In this manner, an organization may be able to bootstrap itself into a position of having its stated spending policy become charter and thus control. See also the discussion in the Commissioners' comments about the retroactive application of these provisions to existing funds.

3.   Rule of Construction

Section 2 does not apply if the applicable gift instrument indicates the donor's intention that net appreciation shall not be expended. A restriction upon the expenditure of net appreciation may not be implied from a designation of a gift as an endowment, or from a direction or authorization in the applicable gift instrument to use only "income," "interest," "dividends," or "rents, issues or profits," or "to preserve the principal intact," or a direction which contains other words of similar import. This rule of construction applies to gift instruments executed or in effect before or after the effective date of this Act.

This section confirms that the donor may override the board's discretion to spend gain. However, it also makes clear that the use of the term endowment no longer means "hold the principal and spend the income" (in the sense of dividends and interest). It also succinctly states that the effect of this law is retroactive.

4.   Investment Authority

In addition to an investment otherwise authorized by law or by the applicable gift instrument, and without restriction to investments a fiduciary may make, the governing board, subject to any specific limitations set forth in the applicable gift instrument or in the applicable law other than law relating to investments by a fiduciary, may:

(1) Invest and reinvest an institutional fund in any real or personal property deemed advisable by the governing board, whether or not it produces a current return, including mortgages, stocks, bonds, debentures, and other securities of profit or non-profit corporations, shares in or obligations of associations, partnerships, or individuals, and obligations of any government or subdivision or instrumentality thereof;

(2) Retain property contributed by a donor to an institutional fund for as long as the governing board deems advisable;

(3) Include all or any part of an institutional fund in any pooled or common fund maintained by the institution; and

(4) Invest all or any part of an institutional fund in any other pooled or common fund available for investment, including shares or interests in regulated investment companies, mutual funds, common trust funds, investment partnerships, real estate investment trusts, or similar organizations in which funds are commingled and investment determinations are made by persons other than the governing board.

The preamble to this section indicates that the powers listed here are subject to certain things and not subject to others. For example, it says that investments are not limited to what a fiduciary may invest in and that the board is investing for its own account, not as a fiduciary for someone else. Plus, anything else permitted by law still exists side-by-side with this law. In addition, the gift instrument may allow (or prohibit) certain things and the board may (or must if a prohibition) follow those items or instructions, including retaining property that may otherwise not be very prudent to maintain.

Note also in (1) that the board may hold property or invest in it with endowment funds even though without a current return on the investment. The comments state that this general provision does not specifically say endowment funds may be invested in the organization's own facilities, but does not prevent it. It appears the drafters believed such investing would be covered by the general clause in (1).

5.   Delegation of Investment Management

Except as otherwise provided by the applicable gift instrument or by applicable law relating to governmental institutions or funds, the governing board may (1) delegate to its committees, officers or employees of the institution or the fund, or agents, including investment counsel, the authority to act in place of the board in investment and reinvestment of institutional funds, (2) contract with independent investment advisors, investment counsel or managers, banks, or trust companies, so to act, and (3) authorize the payment of compensation for investment advisory or management services.

There are two points to note in this section: first, the board can delegate its investment authority to employees or agents such as investment counsel *to act in place of the board with only responsibility for the selection of competent agents (a trustee cannot so completely delegate the investment authority), and second, contract with advisors and counsel for investments. Does this second item permit the charging of fees back to the endowment fund without notification to the donors? Clearly, this also says the donor may by gift agreement override this authority. But will many organizations that have numerous endowment funds and donors want to have differing standards for different donors and agreements? Probably not. This will be a matter of negotiation with the donor or the subject of endowment policies.*

6.   Standard of Conduct

In the administration of the powers to appropriate appreciation, to make and retain investments, and to delegate investment management of institutional funds, members of a governing board shall exercise ordinary business care and prudence under the facts and circumstances prevailing at the time of the action or decision. In so doing they shall consider long and short term needs of the institution in carrying out its educational, religious, charitable, or other eleemosynary purposes, its present and anticipated financial requirements, expected total return on its investments, price level trends, and general economic conditions.

The comments state that this standard is in keeping with the Treasury regulations on investment responsibility for managers of private foundations. The standard is intended to be a business standard. This is intended to apply even if the institution is not in the form of a corporation. It is a standard of care and loyalty and serving the best interests of the entity. It requires weighing and balancing the needs of today against the needs of tomorrow.

7.   Release of Restrictions on Use or Investment

(a) With the written consent of the donor, the governing board may release, in whole or in part, a restriction imposed by the applicable gift instrument on the use or investment of an institutional fund.

(b) If written consent of the donor cannot be obtained by reason of his death, disability, unavailability, or impossibility of identification, the governing board may apply in the name of the institution to the [appropriate] court for release of a restriction imposed by the applicable gift instrument on the use or investment of an institutional fund. The [Attorney General] shall be notified of the application and shall be given an opportunity to be heard. If the court finds that the restriction is obsolete, inappropriate, or impracticable, it may by order release the restriction in whole or in part. A release under this subsection may not change an endowment fund to a fund that is not an endowment fund.

(c) A release under this section may not allow a fund to be used for purposes other than the educational, religious, charitable, or other eleemosynary purposes of the institution affected.

(d) This section does not limit the application of the doctrine of cy pres.

This section is very important and is probably the greatest deviation from the law existing at the time this was drafted. At that time, only the doctrine of cy pres could be applied to change the use of an endowment fund. This required a court petition and proof of general charitable intent as well as the specific intent of the gift. It required a showing of impossibility or impracticability of the use. Then it required a finding of a purpose as close as possible to the original one. This section greatly relaxes the standard if the donor is alive.

There are two distinct rules here. First, if the donor is alive, he or she may release a restriction, even though the donor has no standing to enforce the restriction (the Attorney General has that standing). Thus, the donor merely acquiesces in the change. The donor may not add a restriction.

Secondly, if the donor is unavailable, the board may take it to the appropriate court to release the restriction, but it does not have to show impossibility. It merely needs to show that the use is obsolete, inappropriate or impracticable.

The legal aspects of operating endowment funds are laid out quite well now as opposed to a few decades ago. The UMIFA and case law make it fairly easy to understand. Nevertheless, most administrators and managers the author has met do not refer to this law and just make it up as they go along. It is accessible, easy to read and leaves very few sticky questions open. The accounting rules coordinate fairly well with the legal rules, although there may be some areas of conflict.

Gift Agreements

Whatever you do, when dealing with an endowment gift, write out a gift agreement. Define the terms of understanding with the donor. Even if the donor does not have a property interest in the fund any longer and cannot legally enforce it, the donor can report irregularities to the Attorney General and the news media. Some fine programs have been undone for years because of an Attorney General or a reporter's investigation based on a disgruntled donor's report or complaint.

In addition, many donors of high-level gifts have considerable influence in the community and with your board.

4

Management of the Funds: Accounting Aspects and Investments

Once endowment funds are received, another form of work begins. The funds must be properly accounted for and invested to meet the goals of the endowment gift. While none of the authors is an accountant or an investment advisor, certain issues are well known to those persons who manage endowments or consult to those endowment managers.

While the concept of profit is not prevalent and perhaps not even proper, every nonprofit must be accountable for its assets and income to the IRS, certain state or local authorities and for a public charity, to its general public or constituency. Formerly, a concept called fund accounting was utilized and was essentially the equivalent of making the reporting by nonprofits a conglomeration of reports on funds and fund balances, with no industry standardization across the segments of the nonprofit world. Standardization came slowly and really only emerged in the mid-to-late 1990s with several major pronouncements issued by the Financial Accounting Standards Board (FASB).

Financial Accounting Standards Board

For those readers who do not know the term FASB, a little background is in order. Until the mid-1970s, the board that issued rules or standards for Certified Public Accountants was the Accounting Principles Board of the American Institute of Certified Public Accountants (AICPA). Those accounting principles were known as generally accepted accounting principles, or GAAP. CPAs reporting on the financial statements of clients cannot say that the client follows generally accepted accounting principles unless they follow these rules. Later this board evolved into the Financial Accounting Standards Board, which became involved in the nonprofit world in 1977. The most comprehensive and recent pronouncements of this Board came in the 1990s with four major standards — FASB numbers 116, issued in 1993 and effective for fiscal years beginning after December 15, 1994 (with some exceptions); 117, issued in 1993, also effective for fiscal years beginning after December 15, 1995 (with some exceptions); 124, issued in late 1995, effective for fiscal years beginning after December 15, 1995; and 136, issued in 1999, effective for fiscal years generally beginning after December 15, 1999.

FASB 116 relates to the accounting for contributions received and contributions made and covers many categories of gift, bequest, pledge, in-kind transfer and the like. FASB 117 relates to requirements of fund classification for the financial statements of nonprofits (discussed below) and requires that all nonprofits provide a statement of financial position, a statement of activities and a statement of cash flows, in addition to a statement of total assets, liabilities and net assets. FASB 124 relates to the accounting for certain investments held by nonprofits and establishes standards for reporting for losses where the donor stipulates the investment of a gift in perpetuity or for a specified term. FASB 136 relates to gifts where a donor makes a gift to a recipient organization which accepts the assets and agrees to use those assets or income therefrom on behalf of or for transfer to another entity that is also specified by the donor, requiring in some events the reporting of the assets both as asset and liability.

Intake of the Gift

The first step of the management process is the intake of the endowment gift. Several factors must be considered, the first of which is the effect of FASB 116. It covers unrestricted contributions, current restricted contributions, grants, etc., and also covers the area in which we are concerned, gifts that are not currently expendable, which includes endowment gifts as one of its categories. Endowment gifts are to be reported as revenue into a restricted class of net assets, either temporary or permanent. Thus, from the accounting point of view, the gift must be booked in the correct category of funds, as discussed just below.

In addition, the donor's gift arrangement must be reviewed to ensure whether the gift is intended to go into an existing endowment fund or whether a new one is to be created. To what extent a donor may deliberately cause the organization to create a new fund should be the subject of a stated, written policy for the fundraising staff. Guidelines as to the size of gift and the purpose for expenditure should be considered for the ease of administration and avoidance of duplication of accounting and investment expenditures where an established endowment fund may just as well serve the purpose. If it is an existing endowment fund, it may be one that an individual donor created prior to the gift or a fund in which the gifts of many donors are pooled. If the fund has many donors pooled into it, the portion of the fund that is the donor's gift may be represented by units assigned to the gift. The unitization process, used by an institution with a sufficiently large endowment pool, is based on the value of the gift divided by the current unit value. The initial unit value is set arbitrarily and valuations take place to revalue units for additions and investment gains and losses on a regular, frequent basis, such as every month, if not more often. Investment income is then divided among the donors' accounts by number of units in relation to the total units, and the income is then distributable for the purpose for which the particular endowment fund exists. The distributable amount may itself be restricted as to purpose or unrestricted.

Classification of the Gift

The gift must be classified as to whether it is restricted or unrestricted. These categories of classification came into being with FASB 116 and 117. They greatly simplify what was messy fund accounting and lack of uniformity in classification. FASB 117 defines the terms restricted and unrestricted:

> **Permanently restricted net assets.** The part of the net assets of a not-for-profit organization resulting
>
> (a) from contributions and other inflows of assets whose use by the organization is limited by donor-imposed stipulations that neither expire by passage of time nor can be fulfilled or otherwise removed by actions of the organization,
>
> (b) from other asset enhancements and diminishments subject to the same kinds of stipulations, and
>
> (c) from reclassifications from (or to) other classes of net assets as a consequence of donor-imposed stipulations.
>
> **Temporarily restricted net assets.** The part of the net assets of a not-for-profit organization resulting
>
> (a) from contributions and other inflows of assets whose use by the organization is limited by donor-imposed stipulations that either expire by the passage of time or can be fulfilled and removed by actions of the organization pursuant to those stipulation,
>
> (b) from other asset enhancements and diminishments subject to the same kinds of stipulation, and
>
> (c) from reclassifications to (or from) other classes of net assets as a consequence of donor-imposed stipulations, their

expiration by passage of time, or their fulfillment and removal by actions of the organization pursuant to those
stipulations.

Unrestricted net assets. The part of net assets of a not-for-
profit organization that is neither permanently restricted nor
temporarily restricted by donor-imposed stipulations.

The difference between permanent and temporarily restricted assets, as you may have noticed, is that a permanent restriction
cannot be removed by the expiration of a stated term or by the actions of an organization. The temporary restriction can be removed, at which time the funds become unrestricted. The
wording of these rules is quite free of jargon and understandable.
It also makes it clear that it is *the donor* who causes a permanent or
temporary restriction to apply. The board or other third party
may not cause such restriction.

Board designated restrictions are not viewed as restricted
funds, but as unrestricted funds:

Funds functioning as endowment. Unrestricted net assets
earmarked by an organization's governing board, rather than
restricted by a donor or other outside agency, to be invested to
provide income for a long but unspecified period. A board-
designated endowment, which results from an internal designation, is not donor-restricted and is classified as
unrestricted net assets. The governing board has the right to
decide at any time to expend the principal of such funds.
(Sometimes referred to as quasi-endowment funds.)

Thus, the definition of endowment fund is defined as donor
restricted, and specifically excludes board designations:

Endowment fund. An established fund of cash, securities, or
other assets to provide income for the maintenance of a not-
for-profit organization. The use of the assets of the fund may
be permanently restricted, temporarily restricted, or unrestricted. Endowment funds generally are established by

donor-restricted gifts and bequests to provide a permanent endowment, which is to provide a permanent source of income or a term endowment, which is to provide income for a specified period. The portion of a permanent endowment that must be maintained permanently — not used up, expended, or otherwise exhausted — is classified as permanently restricted net assets. The portion of a term endowment that must be maintained for a specified term is classified as temporarily restricted net assets. An organization's governing board may earmark a portion of its unrestricted net assets as a board-designated endowment (sometimes referred to as funds functioning as endowment or quasi-endowment funds) to be invested to provide income for a long but unspecified period. A board-designated endowment, which results from an internal designation, is not donor-restricted and is classified as unrestricted net assets.

You may note that a distinction is made between permanent and temporary portions of the endowment fund, giving rise to the implication that any endowment fund may be wholly permanent, or partially permanent and partially temporary. This must be ascertained at the outset of the intake process of the gift. The business office must carefully review the restrictions of the donor in the gift agreement. What if there is no gift agreement, but letters in the file and responses to promotional fundraising material? This is one area where the FASB must be read in conjunction with the state's UMIFA, if it has adopted that law. See Section 1, subsection (6) defining gift agreement.

A temporary restriction gives rise to a term endowment:

Term endowment. A donor-restricted contribution that must be maintained for a specified term.

Another important concept to understand is the difference between a restriction and a condition:

Donor-imposed restriction. A donor stipulation that specifies a use for the contributed asset that is more specific than broad limits resulting from the nature of the organization, the environment in which it operates, and the purposes specified in its articles of incorporation or bylaws, or comparable documents for an unincorporated association. A restriction on an organization's use of the asset contributed may be temporary or permanent.

Donor-imposed condition. A donor stipulation that specifies a future and uncertain event whose occurrence or failure to occur gives the promisor a right of return of the assets it has transferred or releases the promisor from its obligation to transfer its assets.

The restriction is specific as to the use of the asset and the condition may or may not be fulfilled by the organization, and if not, it may defeat the gift.

Treatment of Gains and Losses on Endowment Funds

An interesting issue exists with respect to gains and losses. Under uniform *trust* laws, such as the Uniform Principal and Income Act or the Revised Uniform Principal and Income Act, gains and losses on principal are treated as changes to principal unless the trust document states otherwise, or unless the trustee is given discretion to determine that they will be classified as income. In contrast, this set of accounting rules for endowment funds treats gains and losses on investments as unrestricted, including gains on endowment funds, *unless* the donor explicitly states in a gift agreement that gains are restricted (not spendable) or applicable state law prevents the spending of gains. Many states have enacted the UMIFA. If the provisions adopted by the state run parallel to the provisions in the model law, gains are spendable within a prudent standard. Thus, the accounting standard requires gains not required by a donor or by state law to be held as restricted principal to be removed from the restricted category and placed in the unrestricted category. This rule is not acceptable to everyone administering endowment funds and many believe gains should be shown in net restricted assets. In addition, this rule causes some gains to be restricted while others become current unrestricted funds. From the accountant's standpoint, this is laborious tracking per donor or fund.

Where gains are not specifically restricted by the donor or by state law, the rule appears to say the organization must transfer all the realized gain (and unrealized gain if the organization is on a market value, not cost, reporting system) to current spendable income. Does this mean all the gain is currently spendable? If so, this rule is in conflict with the prudent person standard for spending gain stated in the UMIFA, Section 6 which requires the governing body to exercise "ordinary business care and prudence" based on a standard given in the law to spend a portion of the appreciation. Section 2 of the UMIFA states that so much of the appreciation as is prudent may be spent. There are definitely areas of conflict between FASB 117 and the UMIFA.

For example, let's say that a $1,000,000 endowment fund has a realized gain of $50,000. No specific law or donor agreement mentions what to do with gain. For accounting purposes, the gain is transferred out of net restricted assets and into current unrestricted assets. But if the board believes it is prudent to retain half of the gain for a cushion against later potential losses or for needs of this endowment fund, does that retention make the $25,000 a quasi-endowment fund? If so, is that quasi-endowment fund for the same purpose as the original one? Is the usage of the funds "restricted as to purpose?" The answer is unclear. It seems to be one thing under the Prefatory Notes to UMIFA (same purpose) and another (unrestricted) under the FASB.

Treatment of Income on Restricted Endowment Funds

Income on the restricted endowment fund may itself be restricted or unrestricted. If the income is restricted, it is for a stated special purpose. It becomes part of that restricted fund, but may be currently spent in accordance with the spending policy which sets a spending rate the organization will use in making its distributions. The income also may have been restricted to accumulation for a number of years instead of spending. If the income is to be accumulated, it is important to understand the intent of the donor as to whether it remains income or is to be added to principal to enhance the principal value of the fund. Thus, later, if a percentage spending rate is applied, the larger enhanced value will give off a larger distributable amount. On the other hand, if the income was merely accumulated for a time deferral and income (not a percent) is the spending rate, the accumulated income would later be released into current unrestricted funds for expenditure.

Distributable Amounts

As discussed in previous chapters, a spending policy will need to be established at the earliest possible stages of endowment fund-raising. It is imperative to be able to tell a donor what will be held in perpetuity and what will be spent. While boards are prone to fiddling with their definitions of this amount to be spent, they must be advised that once a legal representation is made to a donor, the organization must live up to its promises. There is always a question of who will complain if the board changes its mind as to the amount it can spend. While a donor may no longer have legal standing to sue, he or she may nevertheless complain to the state attorney general, who can, and in some states will, prosecute on behalf of donors, or he or she may complain to other constituents, which may in the long run be more damaging.

Accordingly, adopting a policy that sets the spending rate for all of the funds or various spending rates in accordance with different funds is the first order of business in managing endowment funds. See Chapter 2 for different spending rules that have been reported to NACUBO. Of these, here is the current share of the university and college market that uses each:

Spending Rule	1999	1998	1997
1) all current income,	2.5%	3.6%	3.4%
2) pre-specified percentage of current income,	1.5%	1.9%	2.6%
3) pre-specified percentage of market value,	4.2%	4.2%	5.6%
4) pre-specified percentage of moving average,	72.9%	70.6%	67.9%
5) increase last year's spending by specified percent,	6.3%	6.6%	6.4%
6) decide each year,	4.7%	4.9%	5.2%
7) other rule and	7.6%	7.6%	8.0%
8) no established policy.	0.2%	0.6%	0.8%

One glance at these three reported years will show that al-most all reporting schools have adopted spending rules and many are moving toward the pre-specified percentage of moving aver-age of yearly values. The moving average of yearly values is de-sirable to smooth out fluctuations and volatility of the market, especially if there is one valuation date per year, such as Decem-ber 31 or January 1.

What happens, however, when a percentage, however based, is multiplied by a value lower than the historical dollar amount of the fund? If there is no income and no gain, can the original principal be distributed? It would appear that if the in-vestments are carried at cost, then there is gain, but it is unreal-ized. If they are carried at market, it would be important to know whether they were marked down to market where market is below cost (something organizations do not like to do especially because constituents question the investment judgments). If they are marked to market, it would appear that there would be no gain or income from which to make distributions. If it is a true endowment and the donor did not specify usage of principal, distributions may not be available. If quasi-endowment, the board could decide to distribute any portion it wished. If gain from prior years had been transferred to unrestricted funds, possibly in a quasi-endowment, again the board could use this money as a source of distribution.

In older agreements or funds where income is specified as what is to be distributed, there must be income in accordance with the state law definition governing institutions, such as the UMIFA or principal and income laws such as trusts have. Generally, income is defined as interest, dividends, rents, royalties and annuities. If this income is received, it may be distributable per the agreement with the donor or the governing instrument of the endowment fund.

What if the spending rule provides that a certain percent will be spent, but the board feels that there is sufficient support for a named program (distributions restricted to a purpose)? Can the board determine to withhold distribution or to transfer funds to unrestricted current use? It does not appear that it would meet either with the law if it is UMIFA or with the accounting standards.

Allocation of Expenses

In some institutions, certain fees are charged against the endowment funds. This may be set as a matter of policy for all endowment funds, for a specific fund in its governing documentation or by individual donor agreements. Even indirect overhead may be assessed to a fund, although it is less likely. In any event, any charges that are to be made against an endowment fund should be addressed in information given to donors so there is no confusion or suspicion later that some thing had changed in the way the endowment funds are being managed.

Software and Resources

The accounting for endowment funds is often part of a package for nonprofit accounting. Those packages are typically quite expensive. One company offered information on its endowment accounting system that is freestanding software, not tied to an overall accounting package, for the authors to review. The authors thank this company and invite others to submit their software for any future editions of this book.

EAS, Endowment Accounting System, was developed by Larry Hanson, a former IBM employee and a volunteer for the Glendale College Foundation of the Glendale Community College in Glendale, California. Profits from the sale of the software support the endowment fund of the Glendale Community College. The Windows program provides up to seven spending rates, allows for new endowment gifts and additions, unitization, transfer between funds, assessment of administration fees, distribution amounts, reports, interest tracking, other investment tracking, rates of return and much more. The college website is *www.glendale.cc.ca.us.*

Even for the non-business officer, a few books might help for sticky questions. The *AICPA Audit and Accounting Guide, Not-for-Profit Organizations* is helpful. Another good book is *Streetssmart Financial Basics for Nonprofit Managers* by Thomas A. McLaughlin, published by the Wiley Nonprofit Series. A third excellent and very complete tome is the *Financial and Accounting Guide for Not-for-Profit Organizations* by Gross, Larkin, Bruttomesso and McNally of Price Waterhouse Coopers, also published by Wiley and Sons.

Investments

While this book cannot begin to cover the vast field of endowment investments, and none of the authors are in the investment business, there are some points that should be made about creating and managing the endowment fund.

The first point is that nonprofits often operate with committees and one of the committees is often an investment committee or a finance and audit committee that includes investment oversight. This committee must learn the rules of endowments, both legal and accounting, in order to do the job well. Without understanding what the spending rule is or ought to be, which funds are controlled by donor agreement and which are controlled by state law, what that state law is where applicable and how the return on investments must match the planned spending, which must in turn match the stated objective of the fund and many other interrelated matters, the committee cannot do even an adequate job. Thus, the role of the investment committee and the investment objective can only be effective with sufficient knowledge of the members of the committee and the staff of the organization that assists them. The committee must know the difference between setting investment plans, goals and objectives for current investments, split-interest, life income (trust and annuity) investments and endowments. Each has completely different needs and each must be considered separately. One size does not fit all here.

The second point is that the investment managers who actually implement the investment management and are charged with meeting the investment objective must also understand the stated purpose of the endowment fund(s). Every fund held by an institution may have a different need for income versus growth, timing of distribution and risk/reward.

Taken together, these two points present a continuing challenge to organizations. In the long run, the viability of an institution is based on its long-term financial health. Its long-term financial health must delicately balance the investments of endowment funds with the actual spending based on those investments. Some of the threshold questions have already been addressed in other chapters — such as, what is the purpose of this endowment fund, how much of the annual budget should come from unrestricted earnings of restricted endowment funds, to what degree should the development office stress endowment funds as opposed to operating funds. Here, the question is who should decide how to invest these once obtained and how should those investments be managed? In the view of the authors as consultants, investment committees often spend a large portion of their short time together reviewing past investment returns line by line. Abraham Lincoln is credited with saying if he had nine hours to cut down a tree, he would spend six sharpening his axe. So should the investment committee.

The endowment fund must earn at a greater rate than funds are spent. Just as with any business, including inflation. Thus, the choice of an investment objective to meet a spending need is important. It is equally important to select asset types that comport with the mission of the organization. Most investment committee members are recruited from the business sector and serve as volunteers. They must be trained carefully in the mission and philosophy of the organization so that investments and the asset mix follow the heart of the institution. This concept is intertwined with the hard reality of needing to set a path of risk and reward in investing that meets the operational needs of the organization.

The sharpening of the axe might include open discussions about the true mission of the organization, the actual state of finances, what is happening in the short and long term in the market, what is the likelihood that the development office will be a strong one and be able to attain goals and projections for building endowment funds. Too often the authors see investment committees address one topic — what are other organizations doing? While that may be an interesting question, it is essentially irrelevant to the one asking the question. Organizations are like snowflakes — no two are alike. The needs of the endowment funds of one are completely different than the needs of others. In fact, the needs of one endowment fund may greatly vary from another fund within the same organization.

The role, then, of the committee should include both planning and monitoring. In the planning part, it must learn about endowment rules and the heart of the organization. Then it must select a manager (easy for us to say) that will understand both of these things, set the investment objective to meet and exceed the spending rate and then monitor the activity. The last part is the hardest — making the tough decision to can the investment manager when it is called for, not too soon, and not too late.

This can be summarized more easily than it can be accomplished — set the purpose, set the investment objective to provide enough distributable funds to meet the purpose, set the risk/reward ratio based on the purpose of the endowment fund and the financial status of the organization, select the asset mix, monitor the performance, evaluate the performance, the managers and their style of investing and their ability to communicate, discuss problems and be ready to make necessary changes. If all of us could do all of that effectively with our own funds, we would no doubt be happy. Therein lies the true role of investing for endowment funds — this is a fiduciary role. In other words, each person on the investment committee must act in behalf of the organization as if it were his or her own funds, guarding and conserving them and making them grow for the reason they exist as if these were the funds each of them needed to live on for the rest of their lives, because the organization they represent does have that very need.

One other point to note on investments is that more often than we might like, one or more board members have a conflict of interest in that they wish to have their company provide services for the endowment. Board members and committee members obviously have businesses that may be able to serve the organization. However, sometimes the business is slanted toward one type of investment that may or may not best serve the interests of the whole organization. The factor of personal gain is one that causes ill will on boards and should be exposed and avoided. Interestingly, the person whose firm may be able to provide services may in fact be the best suited for the job because of his or her knowledge of the organization and the nature of his or her business. Nevertheless, it must always be treated with a bit of wisdom and a lot of objectivity, and must be voted on without that member's input or vote. Every potential conflict must be aired and discussed, and every board member must accept a service provided in exchange for compensation with a board or committee member. Logically, a vote to employ the services of a board member's firm may be passed by a majority vote, but a dissenting member's views must be given attention and evaluation.

5

Internal Issues

The Board's Role

One of the more written about, but least understood topics in nonprofit management is the role of the board in fundraising. Many on nonprofit boards do not like to bring up the topic for fear that they will be asked to turn in names of friends and contacts, or to approach their affluent friends for money. Indeed, the authors have sat on boards where this is the case. Often neither the board nor the fundraising staff understands the proper approach to getting board members involved in fundraising. Nevertheless, it is important for the board to understand where gifts and grants fit in the financial picture and to facilitate their receipt. In fact, few boards think in terms of fundraising as part of the financial activity of the organization. Usually, the program (exempt function) revenues and expenses and investment income are the focus of financial discussions and review. But every organization should calculate how much annual revenue is derived from the fundraising effort as compared to the revenue derived from the operation of the charitable program. Two simple fractions can make all the difference in outlook. First, find a set of two numbers: gross *program* revenue over gross total revenue, and gross *gift* revenue over gross total revenue. Then, find net *program* revenue over net total revenue and net *gift* revenue over net total revenue.

For example, if the organization's total gross revenue for a given year is $1,000,000 and of that, the gross revenue from operating the program is $500,000, that fraction would be 500,000/1,000,000, or 5/10. If the gift revenue were $400,000, then the second fraction would be 400,000/1,000,000, or 4/10. The remaining 1/10 may be either investment income or unrelated business income. So 4/10 of the revenue, 40%, comes from gifts.

Based on net figures however, the net program revenue may be only $100,000 after expenses of $400,000 to carry out the program. The net gift revenue may be $300,000, after only $100,000 of fundraising expenses. So, as to the bottom line, net revenues may be $100,000, $300,000 and $100,000 from investments (or UBI). Thus, the gifts are actually providing 3/5 or 60% of the *net* revenue and the program only 20%. If an analysis finds this type of scenario to be true, then the board's duties as to gifts and fundraising should be more compelling. If that extra $100,000 of revenue was in fact income from an endowment already raised and in place, this percentage is even more compelling. Obviously, the purpose of the organization is to carry out a charitable program and not only to do fundraising. Too often, however, the board does not see the real ratios and spends a lot of its effort on trying to cut expenses on the program side to make ends meet rather than trying to provide more revenue from this or other sources. Enhancing the endowment will, of course, work on the increased revenue side.

The underpinnings of board work and where their efforts should be focused are quite often not communicated well to the board. If the board member is serving because of an interest in the charitable program, or if the board member is serving for social/business reasons, he or she needs to learn the broader function and role to be carried out in this volunteer job (and a job it is). A board member has five basic roles to play. Each role has its own level of activity depending on how active the member is, but all roles must be understood and undertaken by all members if a board member is fulfilling his or her duties.

First is the policy role. The entity is generally a corporation and a corporation is an artificial legal being that can only act through its directors, officers and employees or agents. The affairs of the entity are the charge of the directors. The responsibility for operations and activities are the responsibility of the management (officers and management employees). The board must be active in its policy role to formulate policy on which the daily affairs, management and operations may be based. There is no such thing as individual decision at the board level, unless the board has officially delegated responsibility to a director or officer (or other person). The boards acts as a body. Daily management involves individual decision all the time, within the scope of the person's position of authority.

Authority of the full board to act for the entity may be delegated to a committee that acts on behalf of the board, to the extent that the delegation was actually made. Certain decisions cannot be made by committee, and most decisions must be reported to the board and possibly ratified or approved by it. State laws will vary on this issue. The board is ultimately responsible for committee actions.

Second is the legal role. The directors are charged with carrying out the activities of the corporation within the legally granted powers of a nonprofit corporation. Those powers are granted under state nonprofit laws. The board may delegate the management of the activities of the corporation to any person or persons, management company or committee, provided that the activities and affairs of the corporation are managed and all corporate powers are exercised under the ultimate direction of the board.

A director performs the duties of a director, including duties as a member of any committee of the board upon which the director may serve, in good faith, in a manner such director believes to be in the best interests of the corporation and with the care an ordinarily prudent person in a like position would use under similar circumstances (the prudent person standard).

Third is the volunteer role. This is sometimes misunderstood and board members may have a tendency to check their business skills at the door when they enter the nonprofit board meeting. This void is most apparent in the formulation and implementation of strategy. Still today after many articles and books are written about it, the tool of strategic management is not consistently used, especially by small and medium sized not-for-profits. When making strategic decisions, their behavior, when compared to a board of directors of a business entity, especially a medium to large size business, differs. Nonprofit boards are generally larger, with greater use of the executive director, fewer inside directors, limited managerial experience, fixed terms of service, and many trustees ignore the task of discussing policies and accepting the decisions of the executive director or CEO. Larger boards are often used to satisfy a volunteer's desire for nominal involvement while leaving the director in control. Volunteers often work on nonprofit boards for public visibility, business contacts and other social benefits.

In a business entity, inside corporate directors make up approximately 40–50% of for-profit boards, whereas nonprofit boards generally have none or one who would be the executive director. Very few nonprofits permit staff to deal directly with the board. Sometimes boards of directors of non-profits who deal with staff and learn too much about the operation are viewed as meddlers.

A *Harvard Business Review* study reports attendance of corporate directors to be at 90% or better, whereas the attendance of nonprofit directors ranges between 50–60%. It also reports that nonprofit organizations consume more meeting time than for-profit board meetings.

The volunteer role may be viewed as having four subsets: selection of the CEO, review of financial performance, social considerations of nonprofit corporate activities and development and approval of policies for the organization (and possibly procedures to implement them). Donations of professional time and personal contributions are expected.

The fourth is the financial role. Probably the major role of the board is to review the financial performance of the organization so it stays alive and afloat. It is not often indicated to a new person coming on the board that the financial task is one of the more important board activities. An analysis showing the five potential categories of nonprofit revenue and what percentage of this organization's revenue comes from each of the categories should be performed for board training sessions. The board should be expected to devote at least that much of its time to each category. The five categories are: money deriving from the program; investment income; unrelated businesses; gifts from individuals; and corporate, foundation and government grants.

Fortunately the fund accounting that confused many business-oriented nonprofit directors and made it difficult for them to acquire the essential information from financial statements on which they must base decisions has fallen by the wayside. Most nonprofits have moved to standard accounting practices and new FASBs as discussed in the chapter preceding this have set forth new accounting rules for nonprofits.

The last is the fiduciary role. The meaning of the word fiduciary is often lost on board members. So is the concept of stewardship. Fiduciary duty means a responsibility to guard and protect the assets (or person in another context) of another. Money or assets donated to a charitable organization are considered to be held in public trust. The board's fiduciary role is to protect this public trust and to protect the entity. Certain agencies watchdog this fiduciary role of the board of directors of a nonprofit — the state attorney general's office in most states.

The concept of stewardship is one unique to nonprofits. In an endowment seminar in Hawaii, the attendees came up with a definition. First, one participant reported that the word comes from sty ward, or the one who guarded the pig sty from theft, an honorable position in old English times. From there a joint definition evolved — guarding and conserving on behalf of another; communicating to those on whose behalf one "stewards"; more than fiscal responsibility, but to oversee the soul of the organization, its human resources and human needs as well. At a minimum it means that the entity can be no worse at the end of stewardship than it was at the beginning and the goal is to enhance the situation. On a fiscal level, it carries the duties of a fiduciary — loyalty, impartiality, communication, reporting, prudence and capital preservation (including overcoming effects of inflation).

The Board's Role in Endowment Planning

The board actually has to exercise every one of the above five roles with respect to building endowment. First and foremost, however, is the necessity of understanding what the program is and the organization's need for such a program. They need to be receptive to listening to *and* hearing why the organization should have endowment funds. Then, if it agrees, it must exhibit commitment to the program so that it succeeds.

Commitment to the Program

What does commitment mean? Every article written and every speech given regarding the board's role in any of the fundraising programs calls for commitment of the board. However, a good definition of board commitment is rather elusive. A board is not born with commitment, it must be developed; that development is incumbent upon the development officer.

Commitment includes, among other things, understanding, giving support both in terms of time and money and most important of all, making it one's own project. It is important to have an executive director or CEO who is excited about building endowment funds as a long-term project and willing to devote time to the development of it him- or herself. Board presentations or seminars to the board are not always as successful as we would like. Perhaps not enough thought or planning is put into them. The first obstacle to overcome is the need for adequate time before the board. Too often the development officer is given twenty minutes, which is cut down to ten minutes, which is cut down to five minutes during the board meeting. But to lay the blame only at the doorstep of the board is not fair. Too often the presentation is not made to elicit involvement and sometimes involves the less important aspects of fundraising, such as what token items will be given in return for various levels of giving. Quite often organizations plan a board presentation without focusing *why* the topic is being presented. Is it for telling the board how much they must commit financially or time-wise? Or should it be for the purpose of showing how important it is to the entity. The presentation must have a definite communicated purpose to be achieved.

Whether it is introduced by means of a board presentation or otherwise, there are certain things to think through to determine if you can get the board to be committed to the creation or enhancement of an endowment fund. You must be interested yourself, and project the vision and fervor of the project. Also, you should be sensitive to volunteer reaction and adjust to it as you go along. Even more important is that you be simple in your presentation and not waste their valuable time. It is better that you be persistent in shorter doses; communication is a *process*, not an event. No's often come before yes's.

Treat your board member or volunteer as if you were approaching a donor for a gift — be kind and don't bludgeon with commitment. Be gentle and explanatory, no gimmicky presentations, *cultivate commitment* as you would a contribution. Nurture the relationship. Don't demand gifts; let board members learn the program and then come to the conclusion they want to give. Don't make it a necessity of involvement in the program or by insisting on contributions to the program. *Neither of these tactics will result in board involvement or commitment.* It may result in fellow board members being embarrassed if they don't sign up to give to the endowment fund, but in the long run, they won't be committed to the *program*. Just as philanthropy has to be voluntary, so does commitment. Therefore, a process of cultivation towards commitment is essential in developing the board's interest in the new program. It is necessary to get them engaged in some way, even a very minor way: reviewing papers, having lunch, answering a question for you. Be resourceful.

In addition, it is absolutely essential to use board members in line with their personality traits and what they enjoy. To require them to do a specific task, such as soliciting, when that board member doesn't enjoy it, may result in the loss of a board member who may have been very valuable to the organization in another function. Either the board member will become soured on the organization as a whole or completely refuse to work on the major gift effort.

Agreeing on a Plan

The board must feel that it will serve the best interests of the organization to have an actively marketed endowment fund. To do this, it will need to see how to progress toward success. The following steps might be considered. Convince the board of the *bottom line. Nothing sells better than an understanding of what will really come in from these gifts.* Assess the readiness of *organization* and its capacity to handle this program. Set realistic revenue goals and determine expenses realistically so the board understands that you are serious and this is not pie-in-the-sky. Set an endowment campaign strategy that includes the board where possible but does not force them. Get the necessary documentation done and ready so that the office is truly prepared for the first gift.

Marketing

Preparing to launch a new endowment fund or revitalize an old one takes good marketing, both internal and external. Both require an understanding of the "product" to be marketed. Why endowment? Is it prudent to use current resources to establish funding for the future? Should money be spent or accumulated, conserved or consumed? Should this generation shape the future via endowment? Will this smooth out the peaks and valleys of the investment world? (Most boards do not think about building endowment for the needs of 100 years from now, but in the sense of a rainy day fund.)

What percent of the budget should come from endowment? What would today have looked like if an active endowment had been created 40 years ago? How would a successful endowment have affected current policies, attitudes, goals and delivery of the charitable program?

Internal marketing requires reaching all parts of the organization to develop policies, to create advocacy for the program, to educate the entity so it can educate to constituents and to establish the right process for this to happen. It is the board, the management and the staff who must be most convinced that endowment is the right thing to obtain. Their enthusiasm will make the case for endowment.

External marketing comes only after the internal marketing. You cannot go to the public with something not embraced by all of the organization. It just won't work and has shown itself to fail many times over. Only after internal marketing will you go to volunteers and donors. What is marketing but sharing the wisdom of doing something and the strategy for achieving it?

There is a definite trend in donating to designated giving. Does this mean a loss of sense of philanthropy or altruism in our society? Does it indicate a desire to control or is it really a chance to be involved? These are some of the topics to discuss with internally so the thoughts make sense when approaching the outside, the donors. What if they want to restrict a gift to endowment and then restrict the income to a specific purpose? Is that acceptable?

Next, you must have a written marketing plan. Endowment funds may come in the form of planned gifts, but they do not always. So, what is the exchange of values when nothing is given back but a belief that a future must be created? This is what you are selling with endowment funds.

Take this to your constituents, develop an understanding of target markets and communicate to the donors their need to participate, not your need for funds. However, you must be cautious that you don't entertain too many people whose need for individual control causes you to set up several nice, but ineffective endowment funds — ones that lead to no common future, but show off a nice name on a large gift. The individual needs for control must be blended with the community needs. In endowment fundraising, you are often dealing with very successful people and need to market this blend of ego and non-ego in the gift. In the long run, this gift must be compatible with the direction and mission of the organization and please and satisfy the donor.

If the donor is too controlling, he or she may need to look to an endowment substitute, such as a community foundation, a donor advised fund, a private foundation or a supporting organization. Thus, the donor can still support the program without causing the whole program to veer off its course, or the future mission of the organization to change to encompass this person's gift.

Endowment marketing is the best example of the toughest sale of all: selling a concept to someone for nothing in exchange, not even current expenditure they can see. Just a belief they are doing what is right. That is, after all, what philanthropy is.

See also *Marketing Magic for Major and Planned Gifts* by L.S. Moerschbaecher.

The Montana Experiment

By James C. Soft

The Logic

"It is worth noting that Montana's Tax Credit for Endowed Philanthropy is unique in the U.S. No other state has ever offered a similar incentive to encourage endowed philanthropy and planned giving."
— Governor Marc Racicot

A Concern from the Executive Branch

In late 1994, Montana Governor Marc Racicot held a meeting in his home to discuss the issue of endowed philanthropy in Montana. Research had revealed that, although Montana ranked 44th in terms of state population, foundation assets and foundation giving within the state were next to the bottom of the list.[1]

---

[1] See Appendix D, October 1996 letter from the Governor

What could be done to stimulate philanthropy in Montana?

A Task Force was appointed in 1995 to address the issues. In an effort to "jump start" endowment giving in Montana, the Task Force determined that local tax policy would be the place to begin. In view of Montana's high state income tax (due in part to no sales tax), would the public sector (legislative branch) pass tax law that would stimulate the private sector to give to the charitable sector?

In short, the answer was, "NO!" A bill to extend the meager tax credit for contributions to endowment funds died in the 1995 biennial legislative session. But why?

From Failure in 1995

The attempt to pass a tax credit bill for endowed philanthropy in the 1995 legislative session failed. In general terms, the 1995 proposal created a tax credit for up to 50% of an outright gift made by an individual taxpayer (credit not to exceed $500) or up to 50% of an outright gift made by an estate or business corporation (credit not to exceed $10,000). In order to qualify for the tax credit, the gift had to be restricted to a general *endowment* fund of a *community foundation* in Montana.

The failure of the bill can essentially be attributable to three factors. First, time simply ran out. Initially, there was considerable support for the bill in the Senate. However, as the session wore on, the bill was tabled in the House as the 1995 legislature came to a close.

Second, the bill did not enjoy unanimous support from the charitable sector. A number of charities voiced their concerns over the exclusivity of the bill. This perception resulted in an erosion of support from legislators on the House side. Although the 1995 bill was amended in committee to include contributions to endowments of all Montana charities, by then the session was nearing the end. The waning support of the legislators became evident as House Committee and Floor votes favoring the bill became the minority position.

Third, in a sense the bill was fundamentally self-defeating. Generally speaking, endowment fund giving tends to be derived from gifts of capital assets, while current fund giving tends to come from gifts out of cash flow. To reward donors with a credit for smaller gifts to endowment (i.e., $500) would likely siphon badly needed current fund dollars into endowments. As a result an immediate cash flow crises could be faced by the very charities the law was intending to strengthen. This further accented the split in the charitable community since the charities that depend on their annual fund campaign would find immediate fund raising in competition with endowment.

To Success in 1997

Following the 1995 legislative session, the Governor's Task Force On Endowed Philanthropy regrouped by promoting new legislation that would unite the charitable sector, stimulate endowment and compliment current fund giving.[2]

The new law extends a meaningful tax credit which encourages individuals to consider planned gifts of capital assets which, in many instances, increases immediate spendable income that frequently compliments current fund giving! Also, the tax credit is extended to businesses for outright gifts to charitable endowments which enables business to give more for the same out-of-pocket costs. And, the credit is offered on behalf of qualified gifts to *all Montana charities*.

This new law was strongly supported in both the Senate and the House and is uniquely illustrative of Montana's three great sectors (i.e., Government, Private and Charitable) working together for the common good of Montana citizens. Charities perform tasks government cannot perform and everyone in the private sector has experienced the important effects of such philanthropy (e.g., churches, schools, hospitals, museums, etc.). To

---

[2]See Appendix E, November 1996 Proposal from the Task Force

induce major gifts through tax policy is not only wise, but also a necessary investment in Montana's future. Montana's new tax law on endowed philanthropy now speaks volumes about its priorities and views on social, educational and cultural policies as well as charity's important role in these areas.

Creating a Win-Win-Win Situation

The Montana Income Tax Credit for Endowed Philanthropy benefits Montana government, Montana taxpayers and Montana non-profits. It is a WIN-WIN-WIN situation for Montana. The benefits generated are far-reaching and will have a multiplier effect that will impact the state for many years to come. In an effort in encapsulate those effects, promotional and educational materials on the new tax credit law included the following "Six Reasons Why the Philanthropy Tax Credit is Good For Montana."

1. **The Philanthropy Tax Credit helps build charitable endowment.** An Endowment is a permanent fund held by or for a Montana charity whereby only the income and growth is used to carry out the charity's mission. Endowments help Montanans meet ongoing community needs.
2. **The Philanthropy Tax Credit helps "lessen the burden" of Montana Government.** By strengthening Montana Endowments, charities are more capable of resolving social, educational, healthcare, and cultural problems.
3. **The Philanthropy Tax Credit can raise Montana revenue.** A philanthropy tax credit is a one time credit offered primarily for a "planned gift." A "planned gift" is a type of gift vehicle which often significantly increases the spendable (and thus taxable) income of the taxpayer each year for the remainder of his or her lifetime.
4. **The Philanthropy Tax Credit keeps otherwise spent federal capital gains tax dollars in Montana.** A "planned gift" avoids federal capital gains tax which can cost Mon-

tana taxpayers up to 20% of the gain on the sale of appreciated assets.

5. **The Philanthropy Tax Credit keeps future federal estate tax dollars in Montana.** A "planned gift" avoids future federal estate tax dollars which can cost Montana taxpayers up to 55% of the amount used to fund the "planned gift."

6. **The Philanthropy Tax Credit saves Montanans federal income tax dollars.** The Montana Tax Credit for Endowed Philanthropy "induces" Montanans to be generous to Montana charities. Such giving generates meaningful income tax savings on the federal level as well.

The Law

"By working together, pooling our resources and building on our strengths, we can accomplish great things."
— Ronald Reagan

Definition of a Planned Gift

[Montana Code Annotated] **§15-30-165. (Temporary) Qualified endowments credit — definitions.** For the purposes of 15-30-166, the following definitions apply:

(1) "Planned gift" means an irrevocable contribution to a permanent endowment *held by* a tax-exempt organization, or *for a* tax-exempt organization, when the contribution uses any of the following techniques that are authorized under the Internal Revenue Code:

(a) charitable remainder unitrusts, as defined by 26 U.S.C. 664;

(b) charitable remainder annuity trusts, as defined by 26 U.S.C. 664;

(c) pooled income fund trusts, as defined by 26 U.S.C. 642(c)(5);

(d) charitable lead unitrusts qualifying under 26 U.S.C. 170(f)(2)(B);

(e) charitable lead annuity trusts qualifying under 26 U.S.C. 170(f)(2)(B);

(f) charitable gift annuities undertaken pursuant to 26 U.S.C. 1011(b);

(g) deferred charitable gift annuities undertaken pursuant to 26 U.S.C. 1011(b);

(h) charitable life estate agreements qualifying under 26 U.S.C. 170(f)(3)(B);

(i) paid-up life insurance policies meeting the requirements of 26 U.S.C. 170 (15-30-165[1] MCA)

Definition of a Qualified Endowment

[Montana Code Annotated] §15-30-165(2). "Qualified endowment" means a permanent, irrevocable fund that is held by a Montana incorporated or established organization that:

(a) is a tax-exempt organization under 26 U.S.C. 501(c)(3); or

(b) is a bank or trust company, as defined in Title 32, chapter 1, part 1, that is holding the fund on behalf of a tax-exempt organization.

Defining the Tax Credit for Individual Taxpayers

[Montana Code Annotated] §15-30-166. (Temporary) Credit for contributions to qualified endowment.

(1) A taxpayer is allowed a tax credit against the taxes imposed by 15-30-103 or 15-31-101 in an amount equal to 50% of the present value of the aggregate amount of the charitable gift portion of a planned gift made by the taxpayer during the year to any qualified endowment. The maximum credit that may be claimed by a taxpayer for contributions made from all sources in a year is $10,000. The credit allowed under this section may not exceed the taxpayer's income tax liability.

(2) The credit allowed under this section may not be claimed by an individual taxpayer if the taxpayer has included the full amount of the contribution upon which the amount of the credit was computed as a deduction under 15-30-121(1) or 15-30-136(2).

(3) There is no carryback or carryforward of the credit permitted under this section, and the credit must be applied to the tax year in which the contribution is made.

Defining the Tax Credit for Business

[Montana Code Annotated] §15-31-161. (Temporary) Credit for contributions by corporations to qualified endowment. A corporation is allowed a credit in an amount equal to 50% of a charitable gift against the taxes otherwise due under 15-31-101 for charitable contributions made to a qualified endowment, as defined in 15-30-165. The maximum credit that may be claimed by a corporation for contributions made from all sources in a year under this section is $10,000. The credit allowed under this section may not exceed the corporate taxpayer's income tax liability. The credit allowed under this section may not be claimed by a corporation if the taxpayer has included the full amount of the contribution upon which the amount of the credit was computed as a deduction under 15-31-114. There is no carryback or carryforward of the credit permitted under this section, and the credit must be applied to the tax year in which the contribution is made.

[Montana Code Annotated] **§15-31-162. (Temporary) Small business corporation, partnership, limited liability company credit for contribution to qualified endowment.** A contribution to a qualified endowment, as defined in 15-30-165, by a small business corporation, as defined in 15-31-201, a partnership, or limited liability company, as defined in 35-8-102, qualifies for the credit provided in 15-31-161. The credit must be attributed to share-holders, partners, or members or managers of a limited liability company in the same proportion used to report the corporation's, partnership's, or limited liability company's income or loss for Montana income tax purposes. The maximum credit that a share-holder of a small business corporation, a partner of a partnership, or a member or manager of a limited liability company may claim in a year is $10,000, subject to the limitations of 15-30-166(2). The credit allowed under this section may not exceed the taxpayer's income tax liability. There is no carryback or carryforward of the credit permitted under this section, and the credit must be applied to the tax year in which the contribution is made.

The Administrative Rules

The administrative rules which further define and explain the usage of the Philanthropy Tax Credit were a collaborative effort on the part of legislators, development officers and tax professionals. The rules include sample computations of the allowable tax credit for individual and business entity taxpayers.[3]

---

[3]See Appendix F, Administrative Rulings

The Legacy

*"He understands the meaning of life who plants a tree under
whose shade he knows he will never sit."*
— Trueblood

New Endowments Created

Without question, the tax credit for endowed philanthropy
not only generated considerable immediate and future endowment activity, but also stimulated considerable planned giving
activity.

Inasmuch as planned giving (often a viable component in
many financial/estate plans of higher net worth people) is not
usually understood as a conventional element of planning by
the professional community at large, the Montana tax credit law
now obligates professionals to pay closer attention to the tools of
the charitable deferred development trade since an extra tax
credit, in addition to the federal deduction, often makes a
planned gift economically compelling (even in "not so high" net
worth estates)!

In short, the tax credit law brought about the "great awak-
ening" of endowment building and planned giving in Montana!
Prior to the passage of the law, only a handful of public charities
had any kind of a development emphasis on planned giving and
even fewer enjoyed any benefits from their own endowment
funds. Private foundations were few (due largely to the sparse
populace) with little prospect of growth. Subsequent to its passage, over 1,300 new current and future endowments were created in just two years (according to reports done by the Department

of Revenue for the first biennium), many stemming from the vehicles of planned giving.[4]

Commercial Trust Company Stimulus?

Perhaps one of the more interesting statistics has been the impact of the tax credit on trust company activities. The increase in charitable remainder trusts, in just two and one half years, was nearly 250% over *the total of all charitable trusts under management* by trust companies prior to the passage of the law! And, the average size of all charitable trusts under management by the trust companies was over $600,000...an important element for the argument of revenue loss and recovery (to be discussed below) from a state fiscal note concern.

Problems and Concerns

The benefit of the tax credit law was quickly revealed by the actual revenue loss which was nearly twelve times the projected revenue loss prior to the passage of the law. At the time, the Department of Revenue for Montana could only speculate, at best, with regard to the initial and ultimate impact. And, even though

---

[4]In the case of charitable annuities, the endowments are immediate in that the "residuum" of the annuity represents the endowment from a "historic dollar value" perspective (definition as per Uniform Management of Institutional Funds Act...adopted by Montana in earlier years). With regards to charitable remainder trusts and life estate agreements, the endowment is yet future even though a tax credit was given based on the remainder interest at the time the gift instrument was established and funded. The actual size of the endowment would be defined by the gift instrument itself (e.g. whether or not the endowment would be the value of the trust or life estate at time of maturity or whether the "historic dollar value" was deemed to be the present value of the remainder interest at the time the gift instrument was funded.

such a disparity between the actual and projected loss signaled the law's enormous success, the likelihood of making the law permanent (the law contained a sunset provision at the conclusion of five years) was jeopardized by its own accomplishment! It became very important to assess the real economic effect of the law.

The responsibility of the state fiscal analyst's office to report to the legislature, though most important, seemed relatively simple. A computerized totaling of the tax credit line on the tax return would identify the credits claimed. A follow up report to the legislators would enable them to know how expensive this law really was! Or, would it?

To be sure, nearly one half of the credits given by the state were for "planned gifts" which generated no future taxable revenues (i.e., entity outright gifts, life estates, charitable lead trusts and life insurance gifts...see THE LAW above), but what about those planned gifts which generated an ongoing taxable income stream (i.e., charitable annuities, charitable remainder trusts, pooled income funds)? Further, life income planned gift instruments often converted low-yielding, low basis, highly appreciated assets into high yielding gift instruments which generate additional on-going taxable revenues for the state. Since the revenue gain, by encouraging life income planned gifts, was not easily identified on tax returns, nonetheless such would be an important consideration in netting out the revenue impact.

For example, a closer look at the charitable trust activities at the commercial trust companies cited above, revealed a likely, present value, tax gain of three to five times the amount of revenue loss attributable to those very trusts alone.[5] In short, a tax credit for a life income gift would become a revenue generator for local government not only from immediate new taxable revenues from the gift instruments themselves, but also from the on-going multiplier economic effect (see "Six Reasons Why..." cited above). Since this was not quickly seen by the executive branch it

---

[5]It can be reasonably assumed that most charitable trusts are funded with low basis, low yielding growth assets with an average pay out of 7.5% for a twenty year term. The present value of the tax on the trust income stream for twenty years will be significantly greater than the tax credit given up in the year the trust was created.

became important to focus on a collaborative working relationship between the charitable and public sector to emphasize the positive aspects of healthy charities lessening the burden of government *as well as* the real revenue impact!

The revenue loss from the credit has grown by multiples in each of the first four years. In all probability, future legislation will be required to modify the law to control the revenue impact as the rest of Montana's citizens learn of the "good news" of endowed philanthropy in Montana! But, in the words of one of America's favorites, only time will really tell "the rest of the story."

[Ed. Note: In April 2001 the Montana Legislature voted to extend this law with minor revisions for another six years. Several other states are now considering similar measures.]

Appendices

Appendix A: Uniform Management of Institutional Funds Act (1972)

1. Definitions

In this Act

(1) "Institution" means an incorporated or unincorporated organization organized and operated exclusively for educational, religious, charitable, or other eleemosynary purposes, or a governmental organization to the extent that it holds funds exclusively for any of these purposes;

(2) "Institutional fund" means a fund held by an institution for its exclusive use, benefit, or purposes, but does not include (i) a fund held for an institution by a trustee that is not an institution or (ii) a fund in which a beneficiary that is not an institution has an interest, other than possible rights that could arise upon violation or failure of the purposes of the fund;

(3) "Endowment fund" means an institutional fund, or any part thereof, not wholly expendable by the institution on a current basis under the terms of the applicable gift instrument;

(4) "Governing board" means the body responsible for the management of an institution or of an institutional fund;

(5) "Historic dollar value" means the aggregate fair value in dollars of (i) an endowment fund at the time it became an

endowment fund, (ii) each subsequent donation to the fund at the time it is made, and (iii) each accumulation made pursuant to a direction in the applicable gift instrument at the time the accumulation is added to the fund. The determination of historic dollar value made in good faith by the institution is conclusive.

(6) "Gift instrument" means a will, deed, grant, conveyance, agreement, memorandum, writing, or other governing document (including the terms of any institutional solicitations from which an institutional fund resulted) under which property is transferred to or held by an institution as an institutional fund.

2. Appropriation of Appreciation

The governing board may appropriate for expenditure for the uses and purposes for which an endowment fund is established so much of the net appreciation, realized and unrealized, in the fair value of the assets of an endowment fund over the historic dollar value of the fund as is prudent under the standard established by Section 6. This Section does not limit the authority of the governing board to expend funds as permitted under other law, the terms of the applicable gift instrument, or the charter of the institution.

3. Rule of Construction

Section 2 does not apply if the applicable gift instrument indicates the donor's intention that net appreciation shall not be expended. A restriction upon the expenditure of net appreciation may not be implied from a designation of a gift as an endowment, or from a direction or authorization in the applicable gift instrument to use only "income," "interest," "dividends," or "rents, issues or profits," or "to preserve the principal intact," or a direction which contains other words of similar import. This rule of construction applies to gift instruments executed or in effect before or after the effective date of this Act.

4. Investment Authority

In addition to an investment otherwise authorized by law or by the applicable gift instrument, and without restriction to investments a fiduciary may make, the governing board, subject to any specific limitations set forth in the applicable gift instrument or in the applicable law other than law relating to investments by a fiduciary, may:

1) Invest and reinvest an institutional fund in any real or personal property deemed advisable by the governing board, whether or not it produces a current return, including mortgages, stocks, bonds, debentures, and other securities of profit or nonprofit corporations, shares in or obligations of associations, partnerships, or individuals, and obligations of any government or subdivision or instrumentality thereof;

(2) Retain property contributed by a donor to an institutional fund for as long as the governing board deems advisable;

(3) Include all or any part of an institutional fund in any pooled or common fund maintained by the institution; and

(4) Invest all or any part of an institutional fund in any other pooled or common fund available for investment, including shares or interests in regulated investment companies, mutual funds, common trust funds, investment partnerships, real estate investment trusts, or similar organizations in which funds are commingled and investment determinations are made by persons other than the governing board.

5. Delegation of Investment Management

Except as otherwise provided by the applicable gift instrument or by applicable law relating to governmental institutions or funds, the governing board may (1) delegate to its committees, officers or employees of the institution or the fund, or agents, including investment counsel, the authority to act in place of the board in investment and reinvestment of institutional funds,

(2) contract with independent investment advisors, investment counsel or managers, banks, or trust companies, so to act, and (3) authorize the payment of compensation for investment advisory or management services.

6. Standard of Conduct

In the administration of the powers to appropriate appreciation, to make and retain investments, and to delegate investment management of institutional funds, members of a governing board shall exercise ordinary business care and prudence under the facts and circumstances prevailing at the time of the action or decision. In so doing they shall consider long and short term needs of the institution in carrying out its educational, religious, charitable, or other eleemosynary purposes, its present and anticipated financial requirements, expected total return on its investments, price level trends, and general economic conditions.

7. Release of Restrictions on Use or Investment

(a) With the written consent of the donor, the governing board may release, in whole or in part, a restriction imposed by the applicable gift instrument on the use or investment of an institutional fund.

(b) If written consent of the donor cannot be obtained by reason of his death, disability, unavailability, or impossibility of identification, the governing board may apply in the name of the institution to the [appropriate] court for release of a restriction imposed by the applicable gift instrument on the use or investment of an institutional fund. The [Attorney General] shall be notified of the application and shall be given an opportunity to be heard. If the court finds that the restriction is obsolete, inappropriate, or impracticable, it may by order release the restriction in whole or in part. A release under this subsection may not change an endowment fund to a fund that is not an endowment fund.

(c) A release under this section may not allow a fund to be used for purposes other than the educational, religious, charitable, or other eleemosynary purposes of the institution affected.

(d) This section does not limit the application of the doctrine of cy pres.

8. Severability

If any provision of this Act or the application thereof to any person or circumstances is held invalid, the invalidity shall not affect other provisions or applications of the Act which can be given effect without the invalid provision or application, and to this end the provisions of this Act are declared severable.

9. Uniformity of Application and Construction

This Act shall be so applied and construed as to effectuate its general purpose to make uniform the law with respect to the subject of this Act among those states which enact it.

10. Short Title

This Act may be cited as the "Uniform Management of Institutional Funds Act."

Appendix B:
Accounting

AICPA AUDIT AND ACCOUNTING GUIDE
Not-for-Profit Organizations, May 1, 1997

Designated net assets. Unrestricted net assets subject to self-imposed limits by action of the governing board. Designated net assets may be earmarked for future programs, investment, contingencies, purchase or construction of fixed assets, or other uses.

Donor-imposed condition. A donor stipulation that specifies a future and uncertain event whose occurrence or failure to occur gives the promisor a right of return of the assets it has transferred or releases the promisor from its obligation to transfer it assets.

Donor-imposed restriction. A donor stipulation that specifies a use for the contributed asset that is more specific than broad limits resulting from the nature of the organization, the environment in which it operates, and the purposes specified in its articles of incorporation or bylaws, or comparable documents for an unincorporated association. A restriction on an organization's use of the asset contributed may be temporary or permanent.

Endowment fund. An established fund of cash, securities, or other assets to provide income for the maintenance of a not-for-profit organization. The use of the assets of the fund may be permanently restricted, temporarily restricted, or unrestricted. Endowment funds generally are established by donor-restricted gifts and bequests to provide a permanent endowment, which is to provide a permanent source of income or a term endowment, which is to provide income for a specified period. The portion of a permanent endowment that must be maintained permanently — not used up, expended, or otherwise exhausted — is classified as permanently restricted net assets. The portion of a term endowment that must be maintained for a specified term is classified as temporarily restricted net assets. An organization's governing board may earmark a portion of its unrestricted net assets as a board-designated endowment (sometimes referred to as funds functioning as endowment or quasi-endowment funds) to be invested to provide income for a long but unspecified period. A board-designated endowment, which results from an internal designation, is not donor-restricted as is classified as unrestricted net assets.

Funds functioning as endowment. Unrestricted net assets earmarked by an organization's governing board, rather than restricted by a donor or other outside agency, to be invested to provide income for a long but unspecified period. A board-designated endowment, which results from an internal designation, is not donor-restricted and is classified as unrestricted net assets. The governing board has the right to decide at any time to expend the principal of such funds. (Sometimes referred to as quasi-endowment funds.) See also *designated net assets*.

Permanent restriction. A donor-imposed restriction that stipulates that resources be maintained permanently but permits the organization to use up or expend part or all of the income (or other economic benefits) derived from the donated assets.

Permanently restricted net assets. The part of the net assets of a not-for-profit organization resulting (a) from contributions and other inflows of assets whose use by the organization is limited by donor-imposed stipulations that neither expire by passage of time nor can be fulfilled or otherwise removed by actions of the organization, (b) from other asset enhancements and diminishments

subject to the same kinds of stipulation, and (c) from reclassifications from (or to) other classes of net assets as a consequence of
donor-imposed stipulations.

Net assets. Resources whose use is restricted by donors as con-
trasted with those over which the organization has complete control and discretion. Restricted net assets may be permanently or
temporarily restricted.

Spending-rate. The portion of total return on investments used
for fiscal needs of the current period, usually used as a budgetary
method of reporting returns of investments. It is usually mea-
sured in terms of an amount or a specified percentage of a moving
average market value. Typically, the selection of a spending rate
emphasizes (a) the use of prudence and a systematic formula to
determine the portion of cumulative investment return that can be
used to support fiscal needs of the current period and (b) the protection of endowment gifts from a loss of purchasing power as a
consideration in determining the formula to be used.

Temporary restriction. A donor-imposed restriction that permits
the donee organization to use up or expend the donated assets
as specified and is satisfied either by the passage of time or by
actions of the organization.

Temporarily restricted net assets. The part of the net assets of a
not-for-profit organization resulting (a) from contributions and
other inflows of assets whose use by the organization is limited by
donor-imposed stipulations that either expire by the passage of
time or can be fulfilled and removed by actions of the organization pursuant to those stipulation, (b) from other asset enhancements and diminishments subject to the same kinds of stipulation,
and (c) from reclassifications to (or from) other classes of net assets as a consequence of donor-imposed stipulations, their expiration by passage of time, or their fulfillment and removal by
actions of the organization pursuant to those stipulations.

Term endowment. A donor-restricted contribution that must be
maintained for a specified term.

Total return. A measure of investment performance that focuses on the overall return on investments, including interest and dividend income as well as realized and unrealized gains and losses on investments. Frequently used in connection with a spending-rate formula to determine how much of that return will be used for fiscal needs of the current period.

Unrestricted net assets. The part of net assets of a not-for-profit organization that is neither permanently restricted nor temporarily restricted by donor-imposed stipulations.

Appendix C: Agreements

ENDOWMENT RESOLUTION

WHEREAS, the Board of Directors of [NAME OF CHARITY] has reviewed a proposal to establish Endowment Funds to receive contributions from donors where donors have restricted such contributions to endowment, and

WHEREAS, the Board of Directors of [NAME OF CHARITY] believes it is in the best interest of the [NAME OF CHARITY] that it hold such funds and engage in this manner of fund development, and

WHEREAS such fund development will help to further the mission of [NAME OF CHARITY] secure its future financial stability,

NOW THEREFORE BE IT RESOLVED that:

1. The establishment of an Endowment Fund is hereby authorized and ratified.

2. The name of the Endowment Fund program shall be [FUND NAME]. The objective of this fund is to [SPECIFY PURPOSE OF FUND].

3. The [NAME] Endowment Fund shall be the property of [NAME OF CHARITY], owned by it in its normal corporate capacity and subject to the terms of the Articles of Incorporation and By-Laws as amended from time to time. In such capacity, the Foundation shall have the ultimate authority and control over all property in the [NAME] Endowment Fund, and the income derived therefrom, for the charitable purpose as defined in Paragraph Two in this Resolution and further defined in the policies and guidelines to be adopted.

4. The investment objective of the [NAME] Endowment Fund is [SPECIFY].

5. The Board of Directors shall from time to time establish rules, procedures, and policies for the operation and administration of such Endowment Fund including the amount of distribution from the fund to be expended currently and the proper allocation of direct and indirect expenses, by fee schedule or otherwise, attributable to the creation and maintenance of such funds. Such rules shall be communicated to donors in writing.

Date: _____   _____
                                        [NAME], Secretary

BOARD DESIGNATED ENDOWMENT RESOLUTION

WHEREAS, the Board of Directors of [NAME OF CHARITY] has reviewed a proposal that would establish a Board-designated (Quasi) Endowment Fund; and

WHEREAS, the Board of Directors of [NAME OF CHARITY] believes that it is in the best interest of [NAME OF CHARITY] to hold funds functioning as endowment,

NOW THEREFORE BE IT RESOLVED that:

1. The establishment of a Board-designated Endowment Fund is hereby authorized and ratified.

2. The purpose of the Board-designated Endowment Fund is to hold and administer certain funds as if they were endowment funds. Such funds shall be derived primarily from the following sources:

    (a) The President, or his delegate shall be and is hereby authorized to establish any particular gift, not otherwise restricted by the donor, as quasi endowment, and

    (b) The Board of Directors, within its discretion, on an annual basis, may contribute a portion of its annual surplus, if any.

3. The Board-designated Endowment Fund shall be the property of the Foundation, owned by it in its normal corporate capacity and subject to the terms of the Articles of Incorporation and By-Laws as amended from time to time. In such capacity, [NAME OF CHARITY] shall have the ultimate authority and control over all property in the Fund, and the income derived therefrom, for the charitable purposes of [NAME OF CHARITY] and other

purposes as defined in any guidelines and procedures to be adopted.

4. The Board of Directors shall from time to time establish rules, procedures, and policies for the operation and administration of such Board-designated Endowment Fund, including the amount of distribution from the Fund to be expended currently and the proper allocation of direct and indirect expenses, by fee schedule or otherwise, attributable to the creation and maintenance of such funds.

Date: _____   _____

[NAME], Secretary

THE [NAME OF ENDOWMENT] FUND ENDOWMENT GIFT AGREEMENT

This Endowment Gift agreement is made by and between [NAME(S)] ("Donors") and the [NAME OF CHARITY]. Donors have delivered to [NAME OF CHARITY] a deed or other instrument of transfer conveying to [NAME OF CHARITY] the property described in Schedule A, on the following terms and conditions.

1. Pursuant to the Agreement, Donors have transferred to [NAME OF CHARITY] the property described in Schedule A attached hereto, receipt of which is hereby acknowledged by [NAME OF CHARITY], subject, however, to all the terms and conditions set forth in this Agreement.

2. The property described in Schedule A is given to [NAME OF CHARITY] to [CHOOSE ONE: create/ add to] an endowment fund, the name of which [shall be/is] [NAME OF ENDOWMENT FUND]. The principal of this fund shall be held [CHOOSE ONE: in perpetuity/ for a term of X years] and [OPTIONAL: FILL IN IN ACCORDANCE WITH YOUR ENDOWMENT'S SPENDING POLICY: X% / X% based on the average of the prior four years' asset value of the fund / all the income / all the income but in no event any appreciation, whether realized or unrealized] shall be distributed for [CHOOSE ONE: general purposes of the organization as determined in the judgment of the Board of Directors / the following specific purpose as stated in the Board Resolution authorizing the creation of the [NAME OF ENDOWMENT FUND].

3. This endowment fund shall be operated in accordance with the [NAME] Endowment Fund Operating Guidelines and Procedures. The undersigned Donor has received a copy of such guidelines and procedures and by

signing this agreement indicates that [he / she / they] have read and understood them.

4. If at any time in the judgment of the [CHOOSE ONE: Board of Directors / Officer / other person by title or capacity], it is impossible, impracticable or inappropriate to carry out exactly the above purpose in the above manner, a purpose and manner as near as is practicable to the above purpose and manner shall be determined by [CHOOSE ONE: Board of Directors / Officer / other person by title or capacity].

5. [OPTIONAL]:   [NAME OF CHARITY] acknowledges upon the basis of an independent appraisal that the property described in Schedule A has a fair market value of $[X].

6. [INSERT ANY OTHER LANGUAGE SPECIFIC TO THIS GIFT THAT IS NEGOTIATED WITH THE DONOR].

7. This is the only endowment agreement with respect to this endowment gift by [NAME OF DONOR(S)]. Any changes to the terms of this agreement during the lifetime(s) of Donor must be in writing and agreed to by both the Donor and [NAME OF CHARITY].

8. This gift is irrevocable and is intended to qualify for charitable deductions under Internal Revenue Code section 170, 2522 or 2055, as applicable.

9. This Endowment Gift Agreement shall be governed by the laws of the [STATE / COMMONWEALTH] of [NAME OF STATE OR COMMONWEALTH].

IN WITNESS WHEREOF, the Donor has signed and executed the Endowment Gift Agreement and [NAME OF CHARITY], acting herein by its duly authorized officer, has caused this Endowment Gift Agreement to be signed and executed in its name and its corporate seal to be affixed.

DATED: _____

[NAME OF DONOR]

[NAME OF CHARITY]

By: _____

Its: [Title]

SCHEDULE A

Items   Value

Accepted by [NAME OF CHARITY] on _____, _____.

                        By
                               [NAME]

                        Its   [TITLE]

Appendix D

OFFICE OF THE GOVERNOR

STATE OF MONTANA

MARC RACICOT
GOVERNOR

STATE CAPITOL
HELENA, MONTANA 59620-0801

October, 1996

To All Interested Montanans:

In a meeting held in my home in November of 1994, community, business and civic leaders from all over the state met with me to discuss the issue of endowed philanthropy in Montana. That conversation convinced me that Montana lags behind the rest of the nation in terms of endowments to strengthen statewide community vitality.

At the beginning of 1995, I appointed the Governor's Task Force on Endowed Philanthropy to address the lack of endowed giving in Montana. Attached is a legislative proposal that the task force has been developing over the past two years. I appreciate their efforts and am pleased to support this proposal.

During the last legislature the task force developed a proposal to promote endowed philanthropy by seeking enactment of a tax credit to encourage greater giving to endowments. That proposal failed. The task force has spent the past eighteen months examining why the proposal failed and modifying it to make it more acceptable to the legislature. More importantly, a number of the improvements provide an even better incentive to promote community vitality through endowed philanthropy. Specifically, the current proposal avoids competition with fundraising for community charities, while at the same time expanding the incentive for greater savings for community endowments.

Over the past few years it has been my pleasure to visit virtually every community in Montana, and those visits, coupled with the changing levels of support by government, convince me that even greater savings will be needed to ensure the security of our communities in the future. Hopefully, the legislature will see fit to enact the attached proposal or one similar to it to provide the necessary incentives for greater community savings.

Should you have any questions, comments or suggestions on how this proposal can be improved, I would certainly enjoy hearing from you.

Thank you for your interest in the future of Montana's communities.

Sincerely,

MARC RACICOT
Governor

TELEPHONE: (406) 444-3111 FAX: (406) 444-5529

3

Appendix E

CHAIR:
Sue Talbot
MT Community Foundation, Missoula

MEMBERS:
Tom Alfrey
U. S. West Foundation, Great Falls

David Auer
MT Community Foundation, Billings

Kris Backes
Plum Creek Timber Co. Foundation
Columbia Falls

Thomas Berg
United Way of Cascade County
Great Falls

Steve Browning
MT Community Foundation, Helena

Cheri Burns
MT Bankers Association, Helena

Chuck Butler
Blue Cross Blue Shield of Montana
Helena

Bill Cain
MPC/Entech Foundation, Butte

Cathy Campbell
Rancher, Wolf Creek

John Delano
MT Community Foundation, Helena

Tom Elliott
N-Bar Ranch, Grass Range

John Etchart

Andrew Malcolm

Linda Reed
Governor's Office, Helena

Alan R. Kahn
Consultant, Bozeman

Vern Petersen
Central MT Foundation, Lewistown

William B. Pratt
MT Community Foundation, Helena

S. Clark Pyfer (Advisory)
MT Community Foundation,
East Helena

Russ Ritter
Washington Foundation, Helena

Larry Robertson
Natural Resources Conservation Service
Helena

Ted Smith
The Henry P. Kendall Foundation
Boston/Polson

Jim Soft
Yellowstone Boys & Girls Ranch Foundation
Billings

Burt Sugarman
GIANT GROUP
Beverly Hills/Whitefish

Margie Thompson
MT Community Foundation, Butte

Josh Turner
Turner & Associates, Helena

Sherry Stevens Wulf
United Way, Kalispell

CONTACT:
Ti Dahlseide
Governor's Office, Helena
406-444-2436 FAX: 406-444-4339

MONTANA
GOVERNOR'S TASK FORCE ON ENDOWED PHILANTHROPY
... Ensuring a Secure Future for Montana

LC No. 546

A Proposal for
ENDOWMENT INCENTIVE LEGISLATION

Background

In the fall of 1994, Governor Marc Racicot appointed a Task Force to investigate and recommend means of encouraging endowed philanthropy to serve the future needs of Montana's citizens. During the 1995 legislative session, the Task Force sponsored legislation calling for a credit against state income taxes for contributions to certain endowments. The proposed legislation failed, but since then, much time and study has been spent reviewing whether and what type of tax incentive might be effective, as one of several components, to encourage endowed philanthropy in Montana. As a result, the Task Force is recommending to the Governor and the next Legislature that a tax incentive be enacted.

The following proposal, which retains the support of the Governor and the Montana Department of Revenue, incorporates many of the suggestions made by Montanans to earlier drafts.

Recommended Endowment Incentive

A credit against Montana income taxes due would be computed in the amount of 50% of qualifying contributions, up to a maximum $10,000 credit per year per individual for a qualifying *planned gift* and a credit of equal size for an outright gift by an estate or corporation. Qualifying charitable contributions, under the Internal Revenue Code, would be defined as a *planned gift* to any qualified endowment. A qualified endowment would be defined as the endowment fund of any organization incorporated in Montana or established primarily for the benefit of Montana citizens or groups and certified as tax exempt by the Internal Revenue Service. Further, a qualified endowment must satisfy the following three conditions to qualify for the recommended tax credit: 1) the endowment must be irrevocable and permanent, 2) the income granted from the endowment must be directed to recipients in a manner that qualifies for tax deductibility as a charitable contribution, under the Internal Revenue Code, and 3) the endowment's principal, revenue and disbursements must be managed in a manner that guards against erosion by meeting the prudent investor rule.

DISCUSSION

1. Q: *Why is the tax credit being proposed?*
   A: To encourage the establishment and/or enhancement of permanent endowment funds to benefit Montanans.

2. Q: *Specifically, what kind of <u>planned gifts</u> are there and which type qualify?*
   A: As discussed above, the *planned gifts* must be irrevocable and qualify as charitable contributions under the Internal Revenue Code. Further, the document of conveyance and/or acceptance must explicitly restrict the *planned gift* to endowment of the qualifying organization.

   Planned gifts meeting the above criteria could include:
   - Charitable Remainder Unitrusts
   - Charitable Remainder Annuity Trusts
   - Pooled Income Fund Trusts
   - Charitable Lead Unitrusts
   - Charitable Lead Annuity Trusts
   - Charitable Gift Annuities
   - Deferred Charitable Gift Annuities
   - Life Estate Agreements
   - Paid up Life Insurance Policies

   Generally speaking, the above *planned gifts* are used by individuals to make an irrevocable commitment of a principal asset for the future (and sometimes immediate) benefit of charity. In most *planned gifts*, the donor retains the use of asset during his lifetime usually because he can't afford to forfeit the earning power of the asset. Tax incentives, such as the proposed credit, induces individuals to make substantial irrevocable *planned gift* "commitments" now to future endowments, thus helping to grow Montana philanthropy.

3. Q: *What is an <u>endowment</u> and why is it important to enhance endowment giving in Montana?*
   A: An endowment is a permanent fund held by a tax exempt organization where the principal of the fund is not expendable. Only the interest and appreciation earned in an endowment fund can be used for current operations. Endowments are established to help Montanans and meet long-term needs, such as providing a permanent source of funds where the earnings can be used to meet future community needs (for education, arts and culture, social services, economic development, health care, etc.).

4. Q: *Why should planned gifts to <u>endowment funds</u>, as opposed to gifts to annual and other charitable fundraising, be singled out for the credit?*
   A: There are already effective tax incentives for gifts to annual and other charitable fundraising. The Task Force believes that the proposed credit will encourage <u>additional</u> planned giving to permanent funds thereby generating income to supplement funds needed for future operating needs and that this additional giving will not detract from the immediate operating funding needs of Montana's charities.

   Endowments are funded primarily by estate bequests and *planned giving*. Annual gifts meet current needs and tend to fall within a predictable dollar range, while contributions to endowments tend to be larger gifts, often made in conjunction with *planned giving* and estate planning. Endowments also can heighten public confidence in an organization and spur increased giving for current needs. Moreover, *planned gifts* often increase spendable income (which, by the way is taxable and thus a "revenue generator" for government) enabling the donor to have extra income out of which they frequently increase their giving to annual campaigns for current needs. For example, when the State of Michigan enacted a tax credit for gifts to charitable endowments, two independent evaluations found no negative impact on United Way giving in Michigan. In fact, annual giving to United Way actually increased.

5

5. Q: *How does this proposed tax credit differ from the previous proposals by the Governor's Task Force on Endowed Philanthropy?*

   A: It differs in two significant ways. First, the tax credit is no longer restricted to gifts to community foundations. A second major difference is the Task Force's increased emphasis on *planned giving* and its growing concern for the need to maintain current giving. The earlier proposals would have provided tax credits to individuals who might make relatively small contributions ($500 or less) to relatively larger endowments in community foundations. This proposal seeks instead to encourage relatively larger planned gifts (i.e., transfers of savings that were created for either retirement support or testamentary transfer) to relatively smaller public and private tax exempt endowments. The purpose is the same: to increase endowed philanthropy in Montana, but the means are quite different: to encourage greater planned giving in Montana to charitable endowments, without adversely impacting current giving.

6. Q: *Can this credit benefit taxpayers of all income levels?*

   A: Yes. Planned giving is an option available to all taxpayers and it is realistically usable by many if not most of Montana's taxpayers. Planned giving deals with saved assets: homes, personal property, pension funds, etc. Many Montanans own such assets later in their lives at a time when they might consider making a *planned gift* to a charity. However, such giving often does not occur simply because taxpayers are accustomed to making gifts out of income only and not from principal assets. The task force believes that a tax incentive, such as the proposed credit, would provide the necessary additional incentive for taxpayers to consider making a *planned gift* to a qualified endowment out of principal assets which is the primary source for endowment.

7. Q: *Why do we need more and larger endowments?*

   A: The needs of all Montana's communities are increasing while resources to help are diminishing. At the same time, government at all levels is shifting responsibility to local communities and many Montana communities lack the resources to assume these additional responsibilities. They lack the permanent endowments, common in most other states, that can provide a perpetual funding stream for charitable purposes and create a cushion against catastrophe. Expanded permanent endowments can help communities achieve the financial security to devise and implement their own best strategies and solutions, serving as a buffer for maintaining essential services in lean years and enabling communities to begin planning ahead, instead of operating hand-to-mouth.

   In addition to aggregating money, endowments also enable donors to accomplish their charitable goals in communities they know and love; they create and nurture community leadership, and they enable local people to allocate community resources to serve locally determined priorities. Endowments offer a tangible way of enlarging the charitable pie rather than continuing to argue about how thinly it might be sliced.

8. Q: *What is the status of endowed philanthropy in Montana?*

   A: No matter how you measure endowed philanthropy, Montana ranks near the bottom of the 50 states. Montana is home to less than three-hundredths of one percent of all U.S. foundations. We rank 48th in the nation in foundation assets and 49th in foundation giving. Despite our relatively small population (ranking 44th in the nation), demographic and income data suggest that the number and size of our foundations should be significantly greater.

11/27/96

6

Appendix F

Montana's Administrative Rules for Tax Credit for Qualifying Gifts to Charitable Endowments - From Volume 42 of Montana's Administrative Rules [ARM]

42.15.507 DEFINITIONS (1) "Allowable contribution" for the purposes of the qualified endowment credit is a charitable gift made to a qualified endowment. The contribution from an individual to a qualified endowment must be by means of a planned gift as defined in 15-30-165, MCA. A contribution from a corporation, sma business corporation, estate, trust, partnership, or limited liability company may be made by means of a planned gift or may be made directly to a qualified endowment.

(2) "Amenities" are items that enhance the pleasantness or desirability of rental or retirement homes, or contribute to the pleasure and enjoyment of the occupant(s), rather than to their indispensable needs.

(3) "Beneficial interest" is a taxpayer who has a beneficial interest in a business whe they are is either a sole proprietor, partner or shareholder in an S corporation.

(4) "Finished product" means a marketable product that has economic value and is ready to be used by a consumer.

(5) "Gross household income" as defined under 15-30-171, MCA, is further defined as:

(a) all capital gains income transactions less return of capital;
(b) federal refunds received during the tax year to the extent that the amount recovered reduced the claimant's Montana income tax in a prior year; and
(c) Montana state income tax and elderly homeowner/renter credit refunds received

(6) Land ownership surrounding a homestead in excess of one acre but less than 19.99 acres will be computed as follows: total amount of property tax billed on the land, divided by the total acreage to equal the allowable amount of property tax use in the credit calculation.

(a) Land ownership of 20 acres or more must go to the county assessor's office for computation of the allowable amount of property tax used in the credit calculation.

(7) "Machinery or equipment" is property having a depreciable life of more than one year, whose primary purpose is to collect or process reclaimable material or is depreciable property used in the manufacturing of a product from reclaimed materia

(8) "Paid-up life insurance policies" are life insurance policies in which all the premiums have been paid prior to the policies being contributed to a qualified endowment. The donor must make the tax-exempt organization the owner and beneficiary of the policy.

(9) A "permanent irrevocable fund" is a fund which receives or will receive the charitable gift portion of a planned gift or a direct charitable contribution and holds the charitable gift or contribution on behalf of a tax-exempt organization under 26 U.S.C. 501(C)(3) for the life of the organization. The present value of the fund at the time that the donor makes a planned gift or an outright contribution to the fund is not expendable by the tax exempt organization on a current basis under the terms of the applicable gift document or other governing documents. For the purpose of the qualified endowment credit, the fund must be used primarily for the benefit of Montana communities and citizens.

(10) "Present value of the charitable gift portion of a planned gift" is the allowable amount of the charitable contribution as defined in 15-30-121 and 15-30-136, MCA or for corporations as defined in 15-31-114, MCA, prior to any percentage limitations.

(11) "Primarily" means over 50% of time, usage, or other appropriate measure.

(12) "Process or processing" means preparation, treatment, including treatment of hazardous waste as defined in 75-10-403, MCA, or conversion of a product or material by an action, change or function or a series of actions, changes, or function that bring about a desired end result.

(13) "Reclaimed material" is post-consumer material that has been collected and used in a process designed to produce recycled material.

(14) "Recycled material" means a material that can be readily utilized without furthe processing in place of raw or virgin material in manufacturing a product and consist of materials derived from post consumer waste, industrial scrap, material derived from agricultural wastes and other items, all of which can be used in the manufactur of new products.

(15) "Rent" is the amount of money charged to a tenant for the occupying of a dwelling. "Rent" does not include amenities such as meals, housekeeping, nursing care, etc. (History: Sec. 15-30-305, 15-31-501, and 15-32-611, MCA; IMP, Sec. 15-30-165, 15-30-166, 15-30-167, 15-31-161, 15-31-162, 15-32-601, 15-32-602, 15-32-603, 15-32-609, and 15-32-610, MCA; NEW, 1992 MAR p. 2196, Eff. 9/25/92; AMD, 1995 MAR p. 2850, Eff. 12/22/95; AMD, 1996 MAR p. 3148, Eff. 12/6/96; AMD, 1998 MAR p. 183, Eff. 1/16/98; AMD, 1998 MAR p. 1004, Eff. 4/17/98.)

42.15.513 ELIGIBILITY REQUIREMENTS TO HOLD A QUALIFIED ENDOWMENT (1) To hold a qualified endowment an organization must be:

(a) incorporated or otherwise formed under the laws of Montana and exempt from federal income tax under 26 U.S.C. 501(C)(3); or
(b) a bank or trust company, as defined in 15-30-165, MCA, holding an endowment fund on behalf of a Montana or foreign 501(C)(3) organization. (History: Sec. 15-30-305 and 15-31-501, MCA; IMP, Sec. 15-30-165, 15-30-167, 15-31-161, and 15-31-162, MCA; NEW, 1998 MAR p. 1004, Eff. 4/17/98.)

42.15.514 TAX CREDIT AND DEDUCTION LIMITATIONS (1) The credit allowed against the corporate, estate, trust or individual tax liability is equal to 50% of the present value of the allowable contribution as defined in ARM 42.15.507. The maximum credit that may be claimed in one year is $10,000 per taxpayer. A contribution made in a previous tax year cannot be used for a credit in any subsequent tax year.

(2) The balance of the allowable contributions, if not used in the credit calculation, may be used as a deduction subject to the limitations and carryover provisions found in 15-30-121, MCA, or for corporations the limitations and carryover provisions found in 15-31-114, MCA.

Example 1:

Credit Allowed	
Present value of the allowable contributions	$50.
Credit calculation (50,000 x 50%)	$25.
Maximum credit allowed	$10.
Excess Contribution Deduction Allowed	
Present value of the allowable contributions	$50.
Less maximum contribution used in credit computation ($10,000 x 2)	-20,
Balance allowed as an itemized deduction	$30.

Example 2:

Credit Allowed	
Present value of the allowable contributions	$15.
Credit calculation (15,000 x 50%)	$ 7,
Maximum credit allowed	$ 7,
Excess Contribution Deduction Allowed	
Present value of the allowable contributions	$15.
Less maximum contribution used in credit computation ($7,500 x 2)	-15,
Balance allowed as an itemized deduction	$

(3) The contribution to a qualified endowment from a small business corporation, partnership or limited liability company is passed through to the shareholders, partners, or members or managers in the same proportion as their distributive share of the entity's income or loss for Montana income tax purposes. The proportionate share of the contribution passed through to each shareholder, partner or member or

manager becomes an allowable contribution for that taxpayer for that year, and the credit allowed and the excess contribution deduction allowed are calculated as set forth in (1) and (2). The credit maximums apply at the corporation and individual levels and not at the pass-through entity's level for partnerships, small business corporations and limited liability companies.

(4) Deductions and credit limitations for an estate or trust are as follows:

(a) if an estate or trust claims a credit based on the computation of the full amount of the contribution, there is no credit available to beneficiaries;
(b) any portion of a contribution not used in the calculation of credit for the estate may be passed through to the beneficiaries, in the same proportion as their distributive share of the estate's or trust's income or loss for Montana income tax purposes; however, beneficiaries may deduct only that portion of allowable contributions not used toward the credit or deduction claimed by the estate or trust; or
(c) if the estate or trust has deducted the full amount of the contribution, the credit may not be claimed by either the estate, trust or the individual beneficiaries.

(5) At no time can a corporation, small business corporation, partnership, limited liability company, estate, trust or individual be allowed to receive the benefit of both a contribution deduction and a credit from the same portion of a contribution.

(6) The maximum credit that may be claimed in a tax year by any taxpayer for allowable contributions from all sources is $10,000. In the case of a married couple that makes a joint contribution, the contribution is assumed split equally. If each spouse makes a separate contribution, each may be allowed a credit up to the maximum of $10,000.

Example 1:
Assume a married couple makes a joint planned gift to a qualified endowment. The allowable contribution made by the couple is $40,000. That couple is eligible to take a credit of up to $20,000 with each claiming a credit of $10,000.

Example 2:
Assume a married couple makes separate planned gifts to qualified endowments, which result in an allowable contribution of $20,000 for each person. They each would be eligible to take a credit of up to $10,000

(7) A contributor may at a later date name or substitute the particular tax-exempt organization to receive the planned gift. However, the trust document or gift document must provide that the recipient of the charitable gift portion of the planned gift is a qualified endowment as defined in 15-30-165, MCA. (History: Sec. 15-30-305, 15-31-501, MCA; IMP, Sec. 15-30-165, 15-30-166, 15-30-167, 15-31-161, and 15-31-162, MCA; NEW, 1998 MAR p. 1004, Eff. 4/17/98.)

42.15.515 CREATING A PERMANENT IRREVOCABLE FUND (1) A

permanent, irrevocable fund can be created by a restriction in the applicable planned gift document indicating the donor's intention that the contribution shall be held in a permanent, irrevocable fund. For planned gifts other than paid-up life insurance policies, the applicable planned gift document is the trust document, gift annuity contract, life estate agreement or pooled income fund agreement.

(2) A permanent irrevocable fund can be created in a separate gift document accompanying an outright contribution.

(3) A permanent irrevocable fund may be created by either a qualified organization referenced in ARM 42.15.513 under a separate governing document or when a donor creates an endowment through a gift document.

(4) By creating a permanent, irrevocable fund and receiving the credit, the taxpayer waives the right under 72-30-207, MCA, to release the restriction in the gift document.

(5) All funds created by donors or qualified organiza-tions must meet the requirements of a permanent irrevocable fund provided in these rules. (History: Sec 15-30-305, 15-31-501, MCA; IMP, Sec. 15-30-165, 15-30-167, 15-31-161 and 15-31-162, MCA; NEW, 1998 MAR p. 1004, Eff. 4/17/98.)

42.15.516 REPORTING REQUIREMENTS (1) The taxpayer must attach a copy c the following information to the tax return reporting the credit:

(a) a receipt acknowledging the amount of the allowable contribution from:
(i) the tax-exempt organization under 26 U.S.C. 501(C)(3) holding the qualified endowment receiving the contribution;
(ii) from the trustee of the trust administering the planned gift; or
(iii) from the bank or trust company holding a qualified endowment on behalf of a tax exempt organization.
(b) the date of the contribution to the qualified endowment or the planned gift;
(c) the name of the organization incorporated or established in Montana holding the qualified endowment fund or the name of the tax exempt organization on behalf of which the qualified endowment fund is held;
(d) In the case of a charitable trust where the charity is yet to be named, the taxpayɛ shall include a copy of the disposition clause of the charitable trust which gives evidence that a qualified endowment fund has been created; and
(e) a description of the type of gift, i.e. outright gift, charitable remainder unitrust, charitable gift annuity, etc.

(2) The information required by these rules will be reported on forms prescribed an made available by the department of revenue. (History: Sec. 15-30-305, 15-31-501, MCA; IMP, Sec. 15-30-166, 15-30-167, 15-31-161 and 15-31-162, MCA; NEW, 1998 MAR p. 1004, Eff. 4/17/98.)

42.15.517 APPLICABILITY DATES (1) The rules in this sub-chapter which apply to qualified endowment funds are applicable for tax years beginning after December 31, 1996 and to allowable contributions made on or before December 31, 2001.

(History: Sec. 15-30-305, 15-31-501, MCA; IMP, Sec. 15-30-165, 15-30-166, 15-30-167, 15-31-161 and 15-31-162, MCA; NEW, 1998 MAR p. 1004, Eff. 4/17/98.

42.15.518 QUALIFIED ENDOWMENT CREDIT (1) For purposes of the qualified endowment credit, as applied to corporations, the department adopts by reference ARM 42.15.507, 42.15.513, 42.15.514, 42.15.515, 42.15.516, and 42.15.517. (History: Sec. 15-31-501, MCA; IMP, Sec. 15-30-165, 15-30-166, 15-30-167, 15-31-161, and 15-31-162, MCA; NEW, 1998 MAR p. 1004, Eff. 4/17/98.)

Index